IDENTITIES AND FREEDOM

Studies in Feminist Philosophy is designed to showcase cutting-edge monographs and collections that display the full range of feminist approaches to philosophy, that push feminist thought in important new directions, and that display the outstanding quality of feminist philosophical thought.

STUDIES IN FEMINIST PHILOSOPHY

Cheshire Calhoun, Series Editor

Advisory Board

Published in the series

IDENTITIES AND FREEDOM

Feminist Theory Between Power and Connection

Allison Weir

OXFORD
UNIVERSITY PRESS

OXFORD
UNIVERSITY PRESS

Oxford University Press is a department of the University of Oxford.
It furthers the University's objective of excellence in research, scholarship,
and education by publishing worldwide.

Oxford   New York
Auckland   Cape Town   Dar es Salaam   Hong Kong   Karachi
Kuala Lumpur   Madrid   Melbourne   Mexico City   Nairobi
New Delhi   Shanghai   Taipei   Toronto

With offices in
Argentina   Austria   Brazil   Chile   Czech Republic   France   Greece
Guatemala   Hungary   Italy   Japan   Poland   Portugal   Singapore
South Korea   Switzerland   Thailand   Turkey   Ukraine   Vietnam

Oxford is a registered trademark of Oxford University Press in the UK and certain other
countries.

Published in the United States of America by
Oxford University Press
198 Madison Avenue, New York, NY 10016

© Oxford University Press 2013

Library of Congress Cataloging-in-Publication Data
Weir, Allison.
Identities and freedom : feminist theory between power and connection / Allison Weir.
    p. cm. — (Studies in feminist philosophy)
Includes bibliographical references (p.).
ISBN 978–0–19–993686–1 (hardback : alk. paper)—ISBN 978–0–19–993688–5 (pbk. : alk. paper)—
ISBN 978–0–19–993687–8 (e-book)   1. Identity (Philosophical concept)
2. Women—Identity.   3. Liberty.   4. Feminist theory.   5. Foucault, Michel, 1926–
1984.   6. Taylor, Charles, 1931–   I. Title.
BD236.W45 2013
126.082—dc23
2012023592

ISBN 978–0–19–993686–1
ISBN 978–0–19–993688–5

9 8 7 6 5 4 3 2 1
Printed in the United States of America
on acid-free paper

For Nick and Kaelen and Lori and Rebekah

CONTENTS

ACKNOWLEDGMENTS

This book unfolded over the course of several years, and I am grateful for the comments, criticisms, and support of many, many people. In particular, I thank Amy Allen and José Medina for their very thoughtful and generous comments on the entire manuscript. I thank my friends and colleagues in the Philosophy Department and the Women and Gender Studies Program at Wilfrid Laurier University, Canada, where I spent many happy years, and my friends and colleagues at the University of Western Sydney and the University of Sydney, Australia, where I look forward to many more. And I am grateful to everyone who responded to various versions of these chapters at various presentations, and especially to those at the meetings of the Canadian Society for Women in Philosophy, the Association for Feminist Ethics and Social Theory, the Critical Theory Roundtable, and the Colloquium on Philosophy and Social Sciences in Prague.

While completing this book, I received various forms of assistance ranging from inspiration and conversation to institutional and emotional support. I am indebted to Linda Alcoff, Cynthia Willett, Sonja van Wichelen, Amanda Third, Dany Celermajer, Magdalena Zolkos, Mridula Chakraborty, Katherine Gibson, Moira Gatens, Shé Hawke, Shahnaz Khan, Margaret Toye, James Wong, Byron Williston, Rocky Jacobsen, Mecke Nagel, and Mandy Edkins. I also owe thanks to Lorraine Code, Diana Meyers, and Sarah Clark Miller. Lucy Randall at Oxford University Press has provided constant and patient editorial assistance.

I am forever grateful to my extended family of Weirs and Weir relations for a community that has grown stronger and more wonderful every year. Many thanks especially to my siblings, Mike, Greg, Carolyn, and Tom, as well as to David Sugarman for wide-ranging conversations. Again, I thank my parents, Eleanor Sloan and Walter Weir, for more than I can say. I thank Kia and Jerry Waese as well as Sandra Bardocz and Susan Fairbairn for their friendship, support, and inspiration over many years. John Sloan and Litza and Dimitrios Kompridis have provided invaluable support.

My dear friend and colleague, Rebekah Johnston, has sustained my mind and soul and offered very astute critiques, and Lori Spring has been a constant source of loving support and insight, and a lot of laughter. Finally, I thank my fellow travellers, Nikolas Kompridis and Kaelen Kompridis Weir—Nick for his unwavering and enthusiastic support of my work, and for his commitments to receptivity, transformation, and romantic utopianism, and Kaelen for being awesome.

Earlier versions of the first three chapters of this book were previously published as "Who Are We? Modern Identities Between Taylor and Foucault," *Philosophy and Social Criticism* 35, 5, 2009; "Home and Identity: In Memory of Iris Marion Young," *Hypatia: Special Issue on Iris Marion Young* 23, 3, 2008; and "Global Feminism and Transformative Identity Politics," *Hypatia* 23, 4, 2008. A much shorter version of chapter 5 has been published as "Feminism and the Islamic Revival: Freedom as a Practice of Belonging," *Hypatia: Special Issue on Crossing Borders* 28, 2, 2013.

INTRODUCTION

IDENTITIES AND FREEDOM: RETHINKING A PARADOX

If discourse produces identity by supplying and enforcing a regulatory principle which thoroughly invades, totalizes, and renders coherent the individual, then it seems that every "identity," insofar as it is totalizing, acts as precisely such a "soul that imprisons the body."

JUDITH BUTLER, *THE PSYCHIC LIFE OF POWER*

We might, then, more insightfully define identities as positioned or located lived experiences in which both individuals and groups work to construct meaning in relation to historical experience and historical narratives. Given this view, one might hold that when I am identified, it is my horizon of agency that is identified. Thus, identities are not lived as a discrete and stable set of interests, but as a site from which one must engage in the process of meaning-making and thus from which one is open to the world.

LINDA ALCOFF, *VISIBLE IDENTITIES*

I've got more than one membership to more than one club
And I owe my life to the people that I love

ANI DIFRANCO, *IN AND OUT*

The spectre of the prison hangs over any affirmation of identity in contemporary social and political philosophy, as in social and political life. The ideal of identity has developed in modern western culture through a profound ambivalence: while the liberal ideal of freedom offers the possibility of an individuality that is self-made, an identity that is discovered and expressed through the formulation of one's own values and the trajectory of one's own life, this capacity opens us to the danger of entrapment by labels and categories—and worse, by labels and categories not of our own invention, imposed on us by others. The identity of a social collective enables social power and carries the hope of liberation, but it also carries the danger, for each individual, of imprisonment. And with the image of the prisoner, both literal and metaphorical, in *Discipline and Punish,* Michel Foucault conjures a spectre that threatens to engulf us: the modern individual is constituted through disciplinary regimes of power that name and classify, that enable individuation only as they imprison: subjected. In short, identities are both sources and ends of freedom, and identities are the shackles that imprison us.

For feminist theorists, and theorists of gender, race, and sexual orientation, this dilemma is particularly acute, for it is clear that these identities have historically been constituted, at least in part, through relations of power and systems of oppression: through patriarchy, racism, colonialism, and compulsory heterosexuality. Yet social movements for change have historically been grounded in these identities. Feminist, antiracist, and gay and lesbian movements have relied for their existence and power on affirmations of solidarity among women, blacks, and gays: these identities are sources of resistance. While they are critical of identity claims, queer and trans movements too have gained their power through solidarities that rely on shared identities among queer and trans people. Identity politics are effects of relations of power, and they have produced, and continue to produce, struggles for freedom.[1]

In this book I attempt to loosen the knot of identity, to untangle some of the threads of identity that enable our freedom from the threads of identity that imprison us.

My focus here is on feminist theories. While feminism has developed through the affirmation of rights and equality for women, the collective social identity of "women" has been extensively criticized as a category, a claim to sameness or essence, that defines, or misdefines, and constrains us (Riley 1988, Butler 1990) and that, moreover, denies differences and power relations among women (Moraga and Anzaldua 1981, hooks 1984, Mohanty 1987, Anzaldua 1990, Mohanty, Russo, and Torres 1991). Collective identities are seen as sources of retreat and withdrawal into safe homes that shelter us from public life and from recognition of difference (Martin and Mohanty 1986, de Lauretis 1990, Honig 1994), or conversely as traps that inhibit our freedom. Identities are often understood to be founded on a binary logic of exclusion and a policing of boundaries (Butler 1990); and identity politics are then seen as misguided affirmations of the very identities that colonize us (Brown 1995). According to these accounts, identity politics are not a politics of freedom but a self-defeating politics of balkanization, closure, and resistance to change. Many advocate shifting our practices of freedom to performances that subvert identities (Butler 1990), or to action that takes us out of our preoccupation with identities (Zerilli 2005), and shifting our collective struggles to coalitions that do not rely on any claims to identity (Reagon 1983).

All of these arguments are important. Yet even the most impassioned critics of identity recognize that identities cannot be escaped. As social beings, we depend on the construction of identities to create and sustain meaning: our identities allow us to be intelligible to each other and to ourselves, and are the sources of the affective, existential meanings that hold us together, as individuals and collectives. This recognition leads some critics of identity to argue that we are trapped in a paradox. We can't escape them so we must bear our identities as essentially paradoxical: as the subjections that enable. I argue that identities are better understood as complex, rather than paradoxical. Further, I argue that identities can be recognized as sources of important values: of connections to ourselves, to each other, and to ideals; and that these in turn constitute sources of freedom for individuals and collectives. But developing this argument requires taking seriously the critiques of identity, working through these critiques to develop clarifications, differentiations, and reconceptions. This is the project of this book.

In response to the feminist critiques of identity cited above, I argue that understanding identities as sources of freedom requires that we differentiate identity as *category* from identity as *connection to* and *identification with* ideals, each other, and defining communities. Thus, it involves a shift from a metaphysical to an ethical, political conception of identities, and to a focus on practical, ethical, and political identifications as practices of freedom. And this involves differentiating between appropriative identifications and identifications that are transformative: that risk connection, openness to the other, and self-change. Understanding collective identities as sources of freedom requires, further, that we differentiate between identities constituted through denial of difference and identities that are heterogeneous and complex, constituted through difference and conflict. Thus, identity politics can be invaluable sources of resistance when they are practiced not as retreat and withdrawal or policing of boundaries, but as practices that risk the difficult work of connection through conflict, openness, and change. All of this depends on recognizing that identities are not simply effects of a single binary logic of subjection through exclusion, but are produced through multiple contesting relations.[2] Thus, they are best understood not in terms of a paradox of subjectivation but through a recognition of complexity. I argue that identities can be understood as complex webs of interactions among diverse relations of power and diverse relations of meaning, love, and solidarity.

Between Power and Connection

Understanding identities as sources of freedom, then, requires untangling relations of power that subject and subjugate from relations that support us and allow us to flourish. Many theorists understand social identities to be primarily effects of subjugating relations of power, and argue that emancipation requires that for the most part we must be, in Nancy Fraser's words, "weaned from our attachments" (Fraser 1997).[3] Some argue that the constitution of identities through relations of power is paradoxical: our very capacities for agency are produced through the same processes that subjugate (Butler 1999). Other theorists argue that our identities are sources of meaning and social integration, empowerment, and solidarity, and that without them we could not live coherent or meaningful lives, nor could we effectively understand and resist oppression (Moya 2002, Alcoff 2006).

In this book, I draw both on theories of identity as constituted through subjugating relations of power and on theories of identity as constituted through social relations of interdependence, to develop a more complex and nuanced conception of identities as sources of freedom. Both kinds of theories understand individual and collective identities to be socially constituted, but they differ greatly as to what this means. While theories of identity as an effect of power understand the social constitution of identities to be a process of subjection to regimes of power, a range of relational theories focus on the social constitution of individual identity through intersubjective relations, focusing on the role of affect, relations of meaning and dialogue, and the importance of defining communities. While relational theories do consider power relations, and while theories of identity as an effect of power do consider intersubjective relations, each tends to undertheorize the other. I argue for an understanding of individual and collective identities that integrates these two approaches, working through the dichotomies of power and connection to develop a conception of identities and identifications as transformative. I develop an understanding of identities as not simply categories but as connections; this requires a shift from a metaphysical to an ethical and political conception of identities, to an understanding of ourselves as active participants in the constitution of our identities, and to an understanding of practices of identification as practices of freedom.

Through this book, I think through the role of what I call *transformative identifications* in producing and mediating relationships between individual and collective identities. By focusing on the ethical and political role of transformative identifications in the constitution of identities and on the transformative potential of critical relations to defining communities, I argue for an understanding of relational identities that focuses not on withdrawal into safe homes or entrapment in prisons, but on the risk of connection to communities of meaning and communities of resistance. This depends on an understanding of freedom in terms of multiple forms of connection.

Finally, while identity is often understood to be about category, the kind of identity that I am interested in affirming is not primarily about category but about relationship. The central question then is not about sameness. The central question is: to whom and to what am I importantly connected? This question opens up questions about one's history, affiliations, desires, and stories. These are individual questions, but they are also collective: they are about what constitutes us as collectivities, as "we"s in the face of a myriad of differences and conflicts. The stories we tell each other, our desires for and with each other, our difficult and fraught relations to each other, are what hold us together, as individuals and collectives.

Similarly, the kind of freedom I want primarily to affirm is not negative freedom, freedom from interference and constraints. I believe that resistance to oppression is essential for freedom, but I argue that resistance and critique can be developed in the context of a theory of freedom in connection: to oneself, to ideals, to others, to collective "we"s. If the question of identity is "to whom and to what am I importantly connected," the question of freedom is about the nature of those connections: how do the relationships that hold us together constitute not just shackles but sources of freedom?

The Paradox of Identity?

The understanding of identity as paradox is central to the liberal conception of the individual: our understanding of ourselves as freely self-making individuals conflicts with any definition of ourselves in terms of identity categories. And the paradox remains central to poststructuralist formulations in which the identity of the individual and collective subject is always an effect of a subjection that paradoxically enables our agency and our freedom. In *The Psychic Life of Power,* Judith Butler argues that with the metaphor of the soul as prison in *Discipline and Punish*, Foucault forecloses the possibility of resistance, rendering subjects merely docile bodies produced through disciplinary regimes. Butler contrasts this conception of the subject with Lacan's: in Lacanian psychoanalytic theory, while the subject is constituted through the symbolic order of the law, the psyche exceeds the law and normalization. "Identity can never be fully totalized by the symbolic, for what it fails to order will emerge within the imaginary as a disorder, a site where identity is contested" (Butler 1999, 97). In the words of Jacqueline Rose, "there is a resistance to identity at the very heart of psychic life."[4] But while in Lacanian psychoanalysis the possibility of resistance is opened up, it is also foreclosed: psychic resistance remains in the domain of the imaginary, and can never displace or redirect the law. Psychic resistance presumes the continuation of the unalterable symbolic order, and thus the subject remains powerless against the law. (Moreover, if the source of resistance is located in the unconscious, so is conformity: Butler reminds us that our attachment to the law is deeply anchored in our psyches.)

In *The History of Sexuality*, Butler argues, Foucault opens up the possibility of real resistance, not from a place outside the law, but as an effect of power itself. "Foucault's conception initiates a shift from a discourse on law, conceived as juridical (and presupposing a subject subordinated by power), to a discourse on power, which is a field of productive, regulatory, and contestatory relations" (Butler 1999, 99). Here Foucault theorizes power in terms of a "multiplicity of power vectors," and power "not only consists in the reiterated elaboration of norms or interpellated demands, but is formative or productive, malleable, multiple, proliferative, and conflictual" (99). Thus there is a plurality of resistances enabled by power, through "reverse discourses" and "discursive complexities," which are enabled by and exceed the normalizing aims of subjectivation (93).

The idea that agency and resistance can be theorized in terms of multiple contesting and conflicting relations is a tremendously fruitful one, and has the potential to move us out of the trap of the paradox of the subject. But while in these places Butler invokes multiplicity, discursive complexity, and conflict, her own analysis (like that of Foucault in this work) repeatedly returns to a binary model of the law and its self-subversion: even while she writes that Foucault shifts from a discourse on law to a discourse of multiple relations of power, Butler characterizes Foucault's discourse of power in terms of a binary relation between the law and its subversion. Resistance is understood in terms of "the dual possibility of being both *constituted* by the law and *an effect of resistance* to the law" (98). In other words, "the law turns against itself" (100). Thus, the complexity that is momentarily invoked is more commonly reduced to a binary model of law and resistance. The possibility of a field of power vectors and power relations is foreclosed by the paradox of a law that enables as it suppresses, a law that turns against itself.

Butler opens *The Psychic Life of Power* with this description of the fundamental paradox of the subject:

> As a form of power, subjection is paradoxical. To be dominated by a power external to oneself is a familiar and agonizing form power takes. To find, however that what "one" is, one's very formation as a subject, is in some sense dependent on that very power is quite another....Subjection consists precisely in this fundamental dependency on a discourse we never chose but that, paradoxically, initiates and sustains our agency.
>
> "Subjection" signifies the process of becoming subordinated by power as well as the process of becoming a subject. (1–2)

Thus, Butler argues that the formation of the subject is essentially paradoxical—that, in other words, the essence of the subject is paradox. This formulation provides great insight into the mechanism through which our agency is enabled by the very forms of power that subject us. The problem is that Butler extends the model of the paradox of the subject to explain the constitution of every form of self, every form of agency, every form of identity. "The subject is the linguistic occasion for the individual to achieve and reproduce intelligibility, the linguistic condition of its existence and agency" (11). Becoming a self, then, requires that we take on an identity that is produced through subjection to power; and it is this power that enables our agency.

The paradox of the identity of the subject is evident in the image provided by Althusser. Identity is produced by the policeman's call: the call of the law, which names you. Butler stresses that the call always risks misrecognition: the policeman calls, but the call may fail to identify the subject: "The one who is hailed may fail to hear, misread the call, turn the other way, answer to another name, insist on not being addressed in that way" (96). Yet the call is always the call of the law, and agency consists in misrecognition that resists the law. Here again we have lost the possibility of multiple contesting and conflicting relations. For what if the name is called not by a policeman but by a friend or lover? Is the law invoked by the policeman always the source of the name? What if the name was given to us by a parent who loves us, or a community that cares for us? What if we have come up with the name for ourselves together? When we begin to consider these possibilities, we open up real multiplicity—a multiplicity that is closed off by the claim that agency consists in responses to the call of the law.

When the name called is a social category, Butler writes, "what is at stake is whether the temporary totalization performed by the name is politically enabling or paralyzing, whether the foreclosure, indeed the violence, of the totalizing reduction of identity performed by that particular hailing is politically strategic or regressive or if paralyzing and regressive, also enabling in some way" (96). This is an insightful expression of the experience of being trapped by a totalizing identity. But is there any possibility of an identity that is not a totalizing reduction but is open, heterogeneous, fluid, changing? And which is produced by multiple and conflicting relations—of power, and of other kinds of relations?

Butler argues that change and resistance are effects of subversive performances of the law of identity. Thus, the identities "woman" and "queer" are entirely effects of the law, but can be performed in "pathologizing or contestatory modes." Resistance is performed through "a progressive usage that requires and repeats the reactionary in order to effect a subversive reterritorialization" (100). But again, rather than invoking a multiplicity of discourses and "power vectors," these examples repeat the binary opposition of the law and its subversion. Performances can be pathologizing and/or contestatory, and subversion depends on repeating the name of the law, on an iteration in which the law turns against itself. All insight contains its own blindness, and while Butler's insight into the construction of identity through the law that enables is brilliant and compelling, it is also blind to any possibility of an identity that is not, or not only, produced by the law, or that is more or other than a subjugation that enables. While the analysis of the production of subjugating identities is important, it is also important to broaden and complicate our understanding of what identities are.

First, while subjugated identities are produced through subordinating power regimes, not all identities are produced in the same way. The identities and the norms that shape us and identify us are not necessarily subjugating. For example, being French, a sister, a friend, a lover, a student, an activist, a writer, a plumber, are all different kinds of identities constituted in different ways, and they are constituted differently from other identities such as being a woman or Jewish or black or queer. Moreover, each of these identities is constituted differently in different historical and social contexts, and none is constituted in isolation but always in relation to other identities, and identities are not separate and discrete, so that one's multiple identities are not added onto one another but are intersectional.[5]

Secondly, *no* identities are produced *only* through subjugating regimes of power. The meanings of even one's gender, race, and sexual orientation are produced through multiple logics and relations—of power, but not only of power. Understanding these identities requires a more open and differentiated conception of power: the power regimes that subjugate are not necessarily (although they are sometimes) the same as the relations of power that enable. All identities are effects of multiple and conflicting social, economic, historical, and political institutions and discourses. Moreover, identities are produced through various intersubjective affective relations and relations of meaning that interrelate with, and are not reducible to, relations of subjugation. Thus, agency and resistance are enabled not only through turning power against itself, but through multiple kinds of relations and capacities. For example, while the binary of black/white was produced through the colonialist construction of race as a justification for colonization, and is maintained in contemporary racism, one's identity as black is produced not only through this binary but through various and contesting "we"-relations, struggles and solidarities, cultures and traditions, aspirations and interpretations that cannot be reduced to the formula of the law of the name being turned against itself, or of power being deployed in diverse practices.[6] While the identities heterosexual and homosexual were produced in the nineteenth century through the kinds of dividing practices theorized by Foucault, lesbian and gay identities also were and continue to be constituted by practices of self-naming, by solidarities and contestations that are similarly complex and irreducible. The binary of woman/man is, I think, even more complicated, and controversial: certainly it long predates the modern identity formations described by Foucault, and while it is the case that this binary displaces and excludes a multiplicity of possible genders, many theorists argue that the woman/man binary has originated and developed not only through dividing practices of power but also through material relations of reproduction (Alcoff 2006). In chapter 4 I argue that the identity "women" has been and continues to be produced through multiple and conflicting relations.

Thirdly, social identities are always heterogeneous, conflictual, and in process. As José Medina argues, "all identity categories are intrinsically heterogeneous and necessarily unstable" (Medina 2003, 657). Like Linda Nicholson and Cressida Heyes, Medina draws on Wittgenstein to argue that identities can be understood in terms of concepts that are not fixed but produced through complicated networks. Wittgenstein writes: "we extend our concept...as in spinning a thread we twist fibre on fibre. And the strength of the thread does not reside in the fact that some one fibre runs through its whole length, but in the overlapping of many fibres."[7] I argue that this means that identities are produced not (just) through binary logics but through a much more complicated process that is situated and historical. Moreover, it is very often the case that the power regime that subjugates is different from the relations to others and ideals that enable resistance, and the alternative resistant interpretations and practices that empower struggles for freedom.

Finally, I argue that a preoccupation with identities as categories obscures an understanding of identities as *connections* to our ideals, to each other, to places, to our bodies, to ourselves. Once we shift to an understanding of identities as connections, we break open the paradox of a category that constrains and enables, and allow something different to emerge. I argue that it is because they are our connections that identities are sources of freedom. Thus the paradox founded on the opposition between imprisonment and freedom is displaced, and freedom is found not in escape or in subversion, but in the ties that bind us and hold us together.

Saba Mahmood has argued that the focus on the binary of subordination and resistance in feminist theories produces an impoverished conception of agency. Mahmood argues that Butler's analysis of the power of norms "remains grounded in an agonistic framework, one in which norms suppress and/or are subverted, are reiterated and/or resignified—so that one gets little sense of the work norms perform beyond this register of suppression and subversion within the constitution of the subject" (Mahmood 2005, 22). Butler's model of performativity is conceived in terms of "a dualistic structure of consolidation/resignification, doing/undoing of norms" (22). Drawing on Foucault's late work, Mahmood argues for an understanding of agency that moves away from a binary model of subordination and resistance, to think about "the variety of ways in which norms are lived and inhabited, aspired to, reached for, and consummated" (23). Thus, she argues that agency can be understood not only as resistance, but as *inhabiting* norms. This shift in understanding is important, for it allows for a movement out of the understanding of norms as only sources of subjection, to an understanding of agency in relation to norms.

Yet the stranglehold of the paradox model of the subject remains in Mahmood's own work: for even as she criticizes the binary model of the subject in Butler's work, Mahmood grounds her own understanding of agency, in *Politics of Piety,* on the model of "the paradox of subjectivation" that she finds in Foucault.[8] The problem is that Mahmood's critique of the binary of subordination and resistance is focused on the preoccupation with *resistance:* Mahmood argues that feminist theories have failed to question the liberal ideal of freedom, and have thus been unable to theorize kinds of agency that are not focused on resistance or freedom. While this rethinking of agency is important, Mahmood's own preoccupation with resisting the focus on resistance and freedom does not extend to questioning the assumption that norms are necessarily subordinating. Thus, Mahmood understands agency in terms of the paradox of norms that subordinate as they enable. She argues for a conception of agency "not simply as a synonym for resistance to relations of domination, but as a capacity for action that specific relations of *subordination* create and enable" (18; italics in original). Along with Butler, Mahmood conflates norms—and identities—with subordinating laws that paradoxically enable. The difference is that for Mahmood the practices enabled by the norms are not necessarily resistant practices. Thus, Mahmood's critique of the binary model of subordination and resistance does not extend to a critique of the image of the *prison* that is the basis the paradox of subjectivation, but only to the image of *freedom* that Butler holds out.[9] I think this critique is misplaced: I certainly would not want to criticize Butler's focus on a politics of resistance. I would argue that the understanding of the subject in terms of paradox—of a binary logic of agency enabled by subjection—is undercomplex, and distorts not only our understanding of subjectivity and agency, but our understanding of possibilities for resistance, and freedom.

Rethinking Freedom

What explains the hold that the idea of the paradox of identity has upon us? Again we can find clues in Butler's evocative descriptions.

> The desire to persist in one's own being requires submitting to a world of others that is fundamentally not one's own…Vulnerable to terms that one never made, one persists always, to some degree, through categories, names, terms, and classifications that mark a primary and inaugurative alienation in sociality. If such terms institute a primary subordination, or, indeed, a primary violence, then a subject emerges against itself in order, paradoxically, to be for itself. (Butler 1999, 28)

The problem is spelled out quite clearly: one's social identity is constituted through a violent alienation in a world of others, a world that is not one's own. Such a description can powerfully evoke the horror of being cast as an abject, repudiated identity. But this is not what Butler is talking about here. The problem she is describing is the situation of being born into a social world: one is not the author of one's own life, but lives with and is shaped by relations with others who came before. It is sociality itself—life with other people—that is perceived as a primary violence, a primary alienation.

There are other ways to think about this. As Linda Alcoff writes:

> The Other is internal to the self's substantive content, a part of its own horizon, and thus a part of its own identity. The mediations performed by individuals in processes of self-interpretation, the mediations by which individual experience comes to have specific meanings, are produced through a foreknowledge or historical a priori that is cultural, historical, politically situated, *and collective.* In this sense, it is less true to say that I am dependent on the Other…than that the Other is a part of myself. Moreover, one's relation to this foreknowledge is not primarily one of negation; it makes possible the articulation of meanings and the formulation of judgment and action. One's relation is better characterized precisely as absorption, generation, and expansion, a building from rather than an imposition that curtails preferred possibilities. (Alcoff 2006, 45)

In more recent work, Butler is struggling to think about relations to others, relations of recognition, as not always or necessarily relations of subjection and subjugation.[10] But still, in *Giving an Account of Oneself,* the attempt to name one's identity is seen as a response to a "demand to tell the truth" (Butler 2005, 132), a demand for a "complete coherence," a demand that is an "ethical violence," is impossible to satisfy and that produces failure (42). I would argue that the question of identity can be interpreted differently: as a question that opens up stories and images, and allows for, even requires, ambiguity, complexity, and change, as one develops a relationship with another person, with other people, and with oneself. Some of the stories to be told about one's identity are about relations of subjection, but other stories are different. In any case, the connections we create through telling ourselves to each other are what hold us together, and allow us to change, and that is where we can find freedom.

For Butler, identity remains a paradox: "Paradoxically, I become dispossessed in the telling, and in that dispossession an ethical claim takes hold, since no 'I' belongs to itself" (2005, 132). This is the "price that must be paid" in the attempt to name oneself: one's first-person perspective, and one's relation with another individual, are "disoriented" by the social and its norms (25).

But the moment that I realize that the terms by which I confer recognition are not mine alone, that I did not single-handedly devise or craft them, I am, as it were, dispossessed by the language that I offer. In a sense, I submit to a norm of recognition when I offer recognition to you, which means that the 'I' is not offering this recognition from its own private resources. Indeed, it seems that the 'I' is subjected to the norm at the moment it makes such an offering, so that the 'I' becomes an instrument of that norm's agency. Thus, the 'I' seems invariably *used* by the norm to the degree that the 'I' tries to use the norm. Though I thought I was having a relation to 'you' I find that I am caught up in a struggle with norms. But could it also be true that I would not be in this struggle with norms if it were not for a desire to offer recognition to you? (2005, 26)

This is, still, the experience of the (post-) liberal individual who recognizes that one is not the author of oneself, but is conditioned by the language and norms of a social life. This subject is enabled only through being dispossessed: not one's own property. And one is related to norms by being used, rather than using them—as if there were no other relation to norms besides using and being used. The driving force behind the paradox of identity is, then, the liberal ideal of the unencumbered individual who is author and owner of the self, and the ideal of negative freedom: freedom from interference by a social world of norms. Poststructuralist theory recognizes that this is an impossible ideal, an illusion of liberalism; but the ideal persists as the unmourned object of desire. What remains is a melancholic subject, unable to acknowledge the constitutive desire for unencumbered freedom.[11] To do justice to Butler's recognition that some identities are effects of relations of subjection, and to do justice to her understanding of identities as sites of contestation and resignification, then, we need to break open the paradox of subjectivation, and the paradox of identity; to do this, we need different conceptions of freedom. A different conception is offered by Butler herself: "from the beginning freedom has been, not the same as the liberty that belongs to the individual, but something socially conditioned and socially shared. No one person is free when others are not, since freedom is achieved as a consequence of a certain social and political organization of life" (Butler 2009, 128).

In his late work on the ethics of the self, Foucault developed a conception of agency enabled not only through power as the law that produces its own resistance but through an agent's relation to oneself, and to a telos or ideal. Foucault frames the ethical self-relation as a process of subjection, but subjection here is not understood necessarily as subjection to a law, or as subjugation: it is a practice of coming to be a particular kind of self, and depending on the context, and on the substance, mode, technique, and telos of the practice, it can be a practice of subjugation, but it can also be a practice of freedom. Foucault differentiates the analysis of this ethical self-relation from the analysis of relations of power. And this opens up the possibility of relations of self-creation that are not only relations of power. But the ethical self-relation also suggests a different understanding of one way that power works: we are empowered in our relation to ourselves and to a normative ideal. Self-creation, then, is practiced not just through resistance to norms, but through aspiration to norms—through, as Mahmood argues, *inhabiting* norms. This opens up the possibility of freedom in relationship *to* self and to ideals —and to other people. And it opens up the possibility of multiple kinds of power and multiple kinds of relations that constitute the self.

Still, despite this rearticulation of the relation between agency and norms, Foucault continues to regard *identities* as static categories produced through dividing practices that impose sameness. Many contemporary theories of freedom that draw on Foucault continue to conceive of freedom as a practice in opposition to identities, which are understood as static categories. As I argue in chapter 4, Linda Zerilli, following Arendt, similarly reduces identity to a static "what" that is opposed to the freedom of action.

In this book, I argue for understandings of freedom that are developed in and through, rather than against, our identities and identifications. In the chapters that follow I develop conceptions of freedom in relation to others, to the social, to ideals, to ourselves. I argue that freedom in connection is compatible with and often essential to freedom in resistance: identification with defining communities, and with ideals, can be central to resistance to subordination. But the idea of freedom in connection also opens up a different kind of freedom: freedom in belonging itself, or social freedom. I explore the dialectic between these two kinds of freedom—freedom in resistance and freedom in connection—and between two corresponding kinds of identities—resistant identities and identities as connections—while also opening up a diversity of kinds and conceptions of freedom. And I suggest a conception of freedom as the condition of being in relations we can critically affirm.

In the first two chapters, I consider the role of transformative identifications with collective social identities in the constitution and transformation of individual identities. Here, I take up questions of self-knowledge and self-creation, freedom from fixed categories and authenticity, relation to self and a meaningful life. In chapter 2 I argue for a reformulation of identity politics, and this focus is continued in the third and fourth chapters, where I consider the role of transformative identifications in the constitution and transformation of feminist identity politics and of collective identities—in particular, women's identities. In these chapters, I focus on social and political constructions of collective identities through multiple and conflicting relations, and on questions of collective self-constitution and solidarity. In chapter 5, I ask whether a cultural identity that is constituted in opposition to a liberal conception of freedom might be a source of another kind of freedom.

Chapter 1 frames the questions of identity and freedom with an analysis of the opposed theoretical approaches taken by Charles Taylor and Michel Foucault. For Taylor, our identities are constituted, and defensible, through relations to and identifications with specific goods and defining communities. For Foucault, identities (including the deep selves of our subjective experience) are constituted through normalizing regimes of power; thus, we need to shift from a focus on identity to practices of freedom. While it can be argued that Taylor and Foucault are thematizing two very different aspects of identity—Taylor is focusing on first person, subjective, affirmed identity, and Foucault is focusing on third person, or ascribed, category identity—in practice, these two are very much intertwined. I argue that by combining, and moving beyond, these two theories it becomes possible to understand struggles for self-knowledge and for meaning—struggles for identity—as practices of freedom, which involve critical and transformative identifications with defining communities. I argue, following Taylor and contra Foucault, that the development of freedom requires a quest for what Taylor calls authenticity: a pursuit of self-knowledge, through reflection on and affirmation of my commitments and my identifications with defining communities. At the same time, I argue, following Foucault and contra Taylor, that this relation to self requires a continual critique of one's own positions in relations of power, and that this is essential to a practice of freedom through self creation.

Combining a Foucaultian power analysis with a Taylorean understanding of authenticity produces a nuanced account of our capacities for the constitution and transformation of individual identities in the context of identities of race, gender, class, and sexual orientation. Taking Nancy Fraser's and Linda Gordon's example of the "single black mother on welfare" as the "icon of dependency" in America and Charles Taylor's example of the "householder" who understands himself in relation to an ideal of independence, I show that neither individual can develop self-knowledge or freedom without engaging in a practice of connection to self that involves both analysis of relations of power and practical self creation through identification with resistant identities. This requires moving beyond both Taylor and Foucault to an understanding of identity in terms of critical relations with defining communities, and an understanding of freedom through transformation or renegotiation of identities.

While the first part of this chapter focuses on identification with resistant identities as a practice of freedom, the second part develops an understanding of freedom as inhabiting a meaningful life, freedom in practices of connection and belonging: social freedom. The first part focuses on practices of self-knowledge through critical identifications with resistant identities, and the second part focuses on practices of self-creation through practices of belonging. These themes are developed in chapter 2, which draws on Minnie Bruce Pratt's analysis of her own practices of self-change. Pratt develops a resistant identity through practices of self-knowledge and self-creation that depend on critical identifications with multiple defining communities.

Chapter 2 focuses on feminist critiques of the ideal of home as a metaphor for a bounded, safe, and secure identity, and for an identity politics based on a mutually affirming, exclusive community defined by gender, class, or race. Against these critiques, Iris Young argues that that the ideal of home ought to be affirmed as a locus of goods—normative values—that support personal and collective identity: safety, individuation, privacy, and preservation. Yet the feminist theorists Young is addressing—Biddy Martin and Chandra Mohanty, Teresa de Lauretis, and Bonnie Honig—all argue that just these values should be rejected: the ideal of *safety* should be replaced with an openness to risk and danger, the ideal of *individuation* with an acceptance of a non-unified self, the ideal *of privacy*, and autonomy, with a critique of the public/private split, and the ideal of *preservation* with an orientation toward the future, and change.

I suggest that we need to move beyond both critiques and defenses of identity as home, and move beyond the dichotomies that frame this debate, to develop an alternative ideal of home, and of identity, as a locus of values that transcend these dichotomies. Thus, it becomes possible to move beyond the dichotomy of risk and safety to an understanding of home as a place where we take the risk of connection, and take up the challenge of sustaining relationship through conflict. This opens up a conception of identity politics as politics grounded in homes that are sites of resistance, and that are themselves sites of conflict and change. Secondly, we can move beyond the dichotomy of affirmation or deconstruction of the unified self to an understanding of relational identities: identities constituted through both relations of power and relations of mutuality, love, and flourishing. Third, we can move beyond the affirmation and critique of the ideals of privacy and autonomy to an understanding of relational autonomy linked to a conception of home as a ground for freedom. Here, I draw on Cynthia Willett, Patricia Hill Collins, and Toni Morrison, who propose a conception of freedom as the capacity to be in relationships one desires, to expand oneself in relationship. Finally, it becomes possible to move beyond the dichotomy of preservation of the past and orientation to the future with a conception of identity in connection to past and future, through reinterpretive preservation and transformative identification.

While Young's essay focuses on actual homes as sites of individual identity, my analysis develops the connection made by Pratt, between individual identity and identity politics, and between actual homes and the homes of identity politics. Pratt's resistant identity is constituted through both relations of power and relations of love and solidarity: she develops self-knowledge through reflection on the power relations that constitute her, and engages in self-creation through risking connections. This opens up the possibility of a reformulation of identity politics through identifications with loved others, with strangers, and with other resistant identities. This reformulation of identity politics is continued in chapter 3.

Chapter 3 is a reconsideration of identity politics and their relation to feminist solidarity. Drawing on the arguments made in chapter 1, I argue that the dimension of identity as *identification-with* has been the liberatory dimension of identity politics, and that this dimension has been overshadowed and displaced by a focus on identity as *category*. Against the claim that identity politics are based on an assumption of sameness among those who belong to a category, I argue that identity politics are politics of identification: shared interests are not simply given or discovered, but are constructed through our attention to what is significant and meaningful to us. Thus, feminist solidarity plays an important role in constituting women's identity. I argue that feminist solidarity involves identifications with ideals, with a "we," and with each other.

Drawing on work by Chandra Mohanty and Maria Lugones, I address critiques of identification as a ground of solidarity, and distinguish between forms of identification that are appropriative and forms that are transformative. I sketch a political model of identity and identity politics based not in sameness, but in transformative historical process: transformative identifications. I argue that feminist solidarity requires taking the risk of connection, which involves opening up to engagement in conflict and dissent, and thus to self-critique and transformation.

Chapter 4 considers multiple arguments that the category "women" is an effect of the regimes of power that uphold male dominance and compulsory heterosexuality. While these arguments are important, they often produce an understanding of the identity "women" as nothing more than an effect of relations of subjection and ultimately of subjugation. Once "woman" is defined as an effect of subjugation, any call for the emancipation of women ensnares us in what has been called the paradox of freedom: "the category of 'women,' the subject of feminism, is produced and restrained by the very structures of power through which emancipation is sought" (Butler 1990, 2).

I argue that to get out of the paradox we need to change the terms—to broaden and complicate our understanding of what identity is. This requires a shift from a metaphysical to a practical and relational and political conception of identity. We need to move, then, to an understanding of identities as sites of multiple and contested and conflicting (and not just interlocking) relations of various kinds, including not only relations of subjection and subjugation but also relations of recognition and identification, of flourishing, of meaning, of love, of empowerment, and of solidarity. If we understand the identity of women as constituted through multiple and conflicting historical and political relations, we can understand our agency to be enabled not only by relations of power but also by other kinds of relations—not only by the dominant norms that enable as they constrain, but also by norms that contest: norms of alternative and resistant and marginalized cultures and communities. The category "women," then, is not only an effect of power, but also an effect of transformative relations of identification and resistance among and between women.

In this chapter, I draw on Linda Zerilli's argument for a political re-creation of women through women's practices of freedom. Yet, Zerilli frames her argument in terms of an opposition between practices of freedom and preoccupation with identities. Against an understanding of identity as entrapment and freedom as freedom from identity, I argue for an understanding of practices of identification and of transformations of identities as practices of freedom directed toward a community or place where one can belong.

Chapter 5 takes up the conception of freedom as belonging in the context of contemporary debates about cultural and religious identities. In her book, *The Politics of Piety: The Islamic Revival and The Feminist Subject,* Saba Mahmood analyzes the practices of the women in the mosque movement, or piety movement, that is part of the Egyptian Islamic revival. For Mahmood, the study of the piety movement raises crucial questions about the normative liberal assumptions that underlie feminism: in particular, the feminist allegiance to an unquestioned ideal of individual freedom. I take up this question, to ask whether Mahmood's analysis of the agency of the pietists can contribute to a rethinking of freedom. I argue that Mahmood is unable to address this question because of the limitations of the paradox of subjectivation model within which she locates the question of agency, and because she tends to understand freedom only in terms of the liberal model that she criticizes. Mahmood draws on Foucault's late work on the ethics of the self to develop a finely nuanced analysis of the pietists' agency; I draw on this work to develop another understanding of agency, and of freedom: freedom as a practice of connection, or belonging. Through this alternative framework I consider the practices of the women in the mosque movement in terms of several conceptions of freedom: self-creation, positive freedom, communitarian freedom, and critique and resistance. Finally, I suggest that this analysis might help us to cross borders between feminists and other women, and between secular and religious cultures.

In a brief conclusion, I reflect on the conceptions of freedom developed through this book, and suggest that the recognition of alternative modernities will require the acknowledgement of diverse conceptions of freedom.

Notes

1. For an insightful analysis of the histories of identity that have contributed to feminist and Black identity politics in America, see Linda Nicholson (2008).
2. I develop a sustained critique of feminist conceptions of identity as an effect of a logic of exclusion in *Sacrificial Logics* (Weir 1996).
3. Fraser argues, however, for the importance of full political participation of identity groups, as subjected identities, in the public sphere. See Fraser 2010.
4. Rose 1986, 90–91; quoted by Butler 1999, 97.
5. For discussions of intersectional identities see Crenshaw 1991, Lugones and Spelman 1983, Spelman 1988, Moya 2002.
6. For analyses of the development of modern political philosophy through constructions of race, see Mills 1997, Tully 1995.
7. Wittgenstein, § 67; quoted in Medina 2003, 659. See also Nicholson 1994, Heyes 2000, Scheman 2011. I refer to this argument in Weir 1996, 121.
8. In fact this phrase is used by Butler, not Foucault. Foucault does refer to the "paradox of the relation between power and capacities," in "What is Enlightenment?" Interestingly, though, he argues that "the growth of capabilities" must be "*disconnected* from the intensification of power relations." (Foucault 1984a, 48; my italics).

9. Mahmood does, however, suggest a different conception of agency, which is expressed more clearly in a later essay: "It is not due to the compulsion of 'the law' that one emulates the Prophet's conduct...but because of the ethical capacities one has developed that incline one to behave in a certain way." (Mahmood 2009, 78)

10. For a careful and incisive analysis of Butler's struggles to theorize recognition and a critique of her tendency to see relations of dependency as relations of subordination, see Amy Allen, "Dependency, Subordination and Recognition: Butler on Subjection," in Allen 2008.

11. Of course I am referencing Butler's analysis of melancholic heterosexuality, which is, I think, a very insightful and accurate analysis. I am also suggesting, following Eve Sedgwick (1997 and 2003), that Butler's theory of identity is a paranoid theory. But then, so is my reading of Butler.

1 WHO ARE WE?

MODERN IDENTITIES BETWEEN TAYLOR AND FOUCAULT

'These days, it feels to me like you make a devil's pact when you walk into this country. You hand over your passport at the check-in, you get stamped, you want to make a little money, get yourself started...but you mean to go back! Who would want to stay? Cold, wet, miserable; terrible food, dreadful newspapers—who would want to stay? In a place where you are never welcomed, only tolerated. Just tolerated. Like you are an animal finally house-trained. Who would want to stay? But you have made a devil's pact...it drags you in and suddenly you are unsuitable to return, your children are unrecognizable, you belong nowhere.'

'Oh, that's not true, surely.'

'And then you begin to give up the *very idea* of belonging. Suddenly this thing, this *belonging*, it seems like some long, dirty lie...and I begin to believe that birthplaces are accidents, that everything is an *accident*. But if you believe that, where do you go? What do you do? What does anything matter?'

As Samad described this dystopia with a look of horror, Irie was ashamed to find that the land of accidents sounded like *paradise* to her. Sounded like freedom.

ZADIE SMITH, *WHITE TEETH*

Here are two familiar and resonant approaches to the problem of modern identity. For Samad Iqbal, a Bengali immigrant who has lived in London for several decades, identity—an identity shared with others, among whom one belongs—is fundamental to a meaningful life. Its loss leaves one with a vertiginous sense of dislocation, of emptiness. For Irie Jones, a London-born teenager of "mixed race" (her father is working-class English, her mother Jamaican), that kind of identity—an identity of lineage and tradition, of belonging to a past—is an unbearable weight, a constraint; more than that, it has no real, salient meaning for her; it confuses rather than clarifies; it disconnects her from her self. In this chapter I want to examine these two approaches to identity: identity as a source of individual and collective meaning, that enables one to be oneself; and identity as a source of oppressive constraint, as an obstacle to self-creation and a barrier to freedom.

Taylor and Foucault

Charles Taylor and Michel Foucault are arguably two of the most important contemporary philosophers of modern identity, and they offer us two very different descriptions and analyses of modern identities. In *Sources of the Self: The Making of the Modern Identity*, Taylor attempts "to articulate and write a history of the modern identity" (Taylor 1989, ix). In *Discipline and Punish,* and in other work on the regimes of power that shape modern identities, Foucault gives us a very different history and a very different story. I take Taylor and Foucault (and here I am focusing on the early and middle-period Foucault) to be representatives of two philosophical traditions: Taylor's project follows the tradition of interpretation as recollection or restoration of meaning, whereas Foucault's follows the tradition of interpretation as exercise of suspicion.[1] Thus, Taylor is a great builder of edifices, and Foucault is a great unmasker. Paul Ricoeur argues that the tradition of interpretation as recollection of meaning is essentially about *faith*. Postcritical, rational faith, but still: faith (Ricoeur, 28). And Taylor's work is surely an expression of faith in our identities. Ricoeur writes that the three "masters of suspicion"— Marx, Nietzsche, and Freud—are engaged in a kind of "destruction" that is designed to "clear the horizon for a more authentic word, for a new reign of Truth" (29). Foucault, of course, is interested in restoring neither authenticity nor Truth, but he could be said to be attempting to clear the horizon for something better than what we've got.

We can also find Taylor and Foucault in the characters of Samad and Irie: for Taylor, if we give up the very idea of belonging—of identity—then we are left with a world in which nothing matters. For Foucault, if we could move beyond our obsession with identities, we might find something better: we might find freedom. Irie's and Foucault's focus on freedom and Samad's and Taylor's focus on meaning and belonging are entangled and interdependent in important ways. I shall argue that these two approaches can be integrated, not through a paradox of subjectivation model that resolves the tension between them, but through a more complex mapping of the web of identity.

In the first part of this chapter, I argue, following Taylor and contra Foucault, that the development of freedom requires a quest for self-knowledge and a relation to self that Taylor understands as a quest for authenticity: this involves a receptive relation to self and to the "truth" of the self. But this "truth" is, for

Taylor, not an essence but an answer to the question "what matters to me?"[2] At the same time, I argue, following Foucault and contra Taylor, that this relation to self requires a continual critique of one's own positions in relations of power. Thus the "truth" of the self must be understood in terms of a genealogy of historically produced positions in specific relations of power.[3] Taking Nancy Fraser's and Linda Gordon's example of the "single black mother on welfare" as the "icon of dependency" in America and Charles Taylor's example of the "householder" who understands himself in relation to an ideal of independence, I show that neither individual can develop self-knowledge or freedom without engaging in a practice of relation to self and others that involves both analysis of relations of power and identification with resistant identities. This requires moving beyond both Taylor and Foucault to an understanding of identity in terms of critical relations with defining communities. In the second part of the chapter, I focus on the relation between freedom and meaning. I argue that the quest for freedom and the quest for meaning can be balanced only through a conception of freedom in relationship. While the later Foucault shares with Taylor an understanding of freedom in relation to one's own telos, Foucault's work left unfinished the project of finding freedom in relations with others: social freedom.

Self-Knowledge and Critique: Practices of Identification with Resistant Identities as Practices of Freedom

Taylor and Foucault tell two very different stories about the history of modern identities in relation to freedom. In "The Politics of Recognition" Taylor argues that the capacity to discover and create and affirm our own identities developed historically with a liberation from fixed social positions, and entails our freedom and responsibility for the generation of meaning, for self-definition. In *Discipline and Punish* and in *The History of Sexuality,* Foucault turns this familiar story on its head. For Foucault, modern identities are produced by disciplinary regimes that permeate our being, defining and constraining who we are in terms of fixed limits and boundaries of normalcy and deviance. So while for Taylor the modern development of both individual and collective identities corresponds to a liberation from fixed social positions and works to undermine those fixed positions, for Foucault it's precisely the opposite: modern identities are the effects of a deepening and strengthening of domination, which formerly remained above and outside us, and which now is anchored in our very souls.

To some extent, it can be argued that rather than presenting two opposing, and perhaps incommensurable, frameworks for understanding identity,

Foucault and Taylor are actually framing two very different, but related, entities, whose difference should not be collapsed under the single term "identity." Foucault is focusing on third-person, or ascribed, identity, while Taylor is focusing on first-person, subjective, affirmed identity. Foucault is describing the history of identity as externally imposed normalizing classification, or social category. Taylor is describing the development of a kind of identity that is precisely not limited by a category, which is in fact an escape from and resistance to category and classification, because it focuses on questions of existential meaning. When Taylor talks about a modern freedom for self-generation of identity, he is not talking about the generation of normalizing categories. He is talking about our focus on existential questions. When we ask, "who am I?" and "what matters to me?" we're not typically asking questions about category and classification. We're asking questions about desire and meaning and ideals: what do I want, what do I value, what matters to me, what kind of person do I want to be, what is the point of my being here, who am I really?

> What does answer this question for us is an understanding of what is of crucial importance to us. To know who I am is a species of knowing where I stand. My identity is defined by the commitments and identifications which provide the frame or horizon within which I can try to determine from case to case what is good, or valuable, or what ought to be done, or what I endorse or oppose. In other words, it is the horizon within which I am capable of taking a stand. (Taylor 1989, 27)

These are ethical questions about the meaning and value of life, and of my life in particular. Because these are questions about *my* values and ideals, my attachments, and what makes life meaningful for me, these are intensely personal, subjective questions, quite distinct from questions of social category.

But Foucault argues, and demonstrates quite clearly in his genealogies, that when we modern subjects ask "who am I?" and engage in the process of self-interrogation that this question demands, the self we discover is necessarily the sedimentation of normalizing and coercive regimes of power. The very posing of the question "what matters to me" as a question of my *identity* is not only specifically modern (as it is, for Taylor); it is the specifically modern demand, made by specifically modern regimes of power, that I engage as an active agent in a constant process of self-analysis, to discover the truth of myself, to classify myself in terms of social categories. My deepest desires, my core values, must be examined, to determine whether I am normal or deviant.

The modern individual is produced through the disciplines in which he is "described, judged, measured, compared with others, in his very individuality; and it is also the individual who has to be trained or corrected, classified, normalized, excluded" (1979, 191). And the modern individual is an active agent in this process.

For Taylor, the existential question "who am I?" constitutes a quest for *authenticity*. For Foucault, the idea that we can discover our authentic, or true, selves is the illusion of modernity. For Foucault, there is no pregiven objective truth of the self. We are historical beings, and our selves—including the deep selves of modernity—are historically produced. But for Taylor, the ideal of authenticity does not presume a fixed, pregiven self. For Taylor, the ideal of authenticity is not about the metaphysics of substance, or about metaphysics at all, but is, rather, about ethics and an ethical relation to self. The question "who am I?" is a question about my *goods:* what matters to me, what constitutes a good life, for me. For Taylor, this question demands that one develop an authentic *relationship* to oneself, to others, and to ideals and values. The ideal of an authentic relation to oneself is an ideal of being true to oneself, to one's own particularity and uniqueness. There is a truth dimension here, and a moral dimension. One's inner voice and inner feelings are important, because they tell us what is the right thing to do. In other words, one has a moral responsibility to oneself, which is comparable to one's responsibility to others. But note here that the point of the truth dimension is to be true *to* oneself. What matters is that I engage in and commit to a relationship of integrity with myself; that I engage in what could be called, in Foucaultian terms, the care of the self, in a specifically modern way: I must be attentive and receptive to myself, listen to myself, respect and foster my uniqueness and originality. If I don't do this, "I miss the point of my life; I miss what being human is for *me*" (Taylor, 1992, 30). I miss the meaning of my life. The modern ideal of authenticity, then, accords moral importance to a particular kind of relation to oneself.

This relationship does also require that I struggle to discover and respect the truth *of* myself. But Taylor is fully aware that this quest and this truth are *social* and *historical.* The need to discover and define one's own meaning, and the belief that one can do so, are specific to modern western culture. And Taylor agrees with Foucault that the idea of the pregiven inner core or fixed truth of the self is a modern illusion. For Taylor, it is an illusion that we can discover a self that is not socially constituted, that we can find a true individual identity distinct from the false identities produced through social meanings and constructions. Taylor argues that the monological conception of the inner self as an essential truth, which one has only to discover by looking inward, is wrong. But he does not believe that that misconception invalidates the ideal of authenticity. Taylor argues that we are essentially dialogical beings. We define our identities through relationships with (and struggles against) others—and ourselves. And we define ourselves always in linguistic and cultural contexts of meaning. For Taylor, then, the self to which we are related is, to its core, a dialogical self, dependent on dialogue, on relations of recognition and mis-recognition with others, on background meanings and languages, and always in a process of change through dialogue, through relationship and interaction with others and with the world. Far from discovering a true self in isolation from society, we can only be ourselves and relate to ourselves through embed-dedness in communities and background horizons of meaning.

Authenticity, however, remains an ideal for Taylor, because as dialogical beings we ask existential questions about who we are, about the meaning and value of our lives, because it is up to us to discover and create those meanings through dialogue and reflection, and because we can only do this through a relationship of integrity with ourselves. Moreover, because we are dialogical beings, the question "who am I?" is always and necessarily linked to the question "who are we?" We need to understand ourselves in terms of shared identities and associations that give meaning and signifi-cance to our lives. In *Sources of the Self,* Taylor argues that our identities are composed of two dimensions: our commitments to our values, and our attachments to "defining communities" (Taylor, 1989, 36). In "The Politics of Recognition" he argues that this means that we are always participants in struggles for definition and recognition of both our individual and our collective identities.

Again, Foucault tells a very different story. For Foucault, when we go looking for our selves and our meanings, what we find are identity catego-ries produced through power/knowledge regimes, which serve to delineate boundaries between normalcy and deviance, and to police those boundar-ies through mechanisms of self-surveillance. So not only what we take to be social categories (e.g., black and white, gay and straight) but also identities of character, and of what we understand to be our deep selves, are produced as binary categories, and human beings must constantly struggle to live up to (and resist) their terms. Thus for Foucault the ideal of authenticity, rather than undermining fixed social identities, effectively elevates them to the sta-tus of essential truth of the self. Rather than escaping fixed social positions, we have come to be the kind of beings who believe there are fixed identi-ties that define our character. Nancy Fraser and Linda Gordon make this point very clearly in their essay, "A Genealogy of 'Dependency'": whereas in the preindustrial period in Europe it was recognized that most of us live in relations of dependency, now we have designated certain groups of people—specifically, people who don't work for money, and paradigmatically, "single black mothers on welfare"—as essentially dependent, and therefore deviant from the norm of independence.

And while questions of category are conceptually different from questions of existential meaning, the two kinds of questions do get mixed up with each other in practice. If I am a black single mother on welfare trying to understand who I am and who I want to be, it will be difficult for me to escape an understanding of myself as a dependent person, and difficult to resist a desire to become more "independent" by getting off welfare, getting my kids into day care and getting a job, however low paying.

Foucault, then, is right to focus on the ways that social categories are imported into our deepest self-understandings, and to note that the ideal of authenticity can serve to anchor regimes of power in the self.

On the other hand, if I am a single black woman on welfare, my questions about who I am and who I want to be will also be framed by competing and conflicting social interpretations—for instance, black communities' valuations of black cultures and analyses of racism, Afrocentric models of community, black women's cultures of resistance, images of strong black women, popular idealizations of motherhood, feminist arguments that mothering work is deserving of social support, left critiques of the capitalist welfare state. My capacity to criticize dominant social constructions of myself will depend to a large extent on my capacity to access alternative interpretations. Those alternative interpretations frame alternative identities—in this case, *resistant* identities. And my capacity to access these alternative interpretations will depend to a large extent on my *identifications with* those alternative, resistant identities—in this case, with black, feminist, left communities of resistance. Foucault does recognize the existence of resistant "subjugated knowledges" (1980b, 82), but he does not go on to recognize that resistant knowledges and competing discourses produce resistant and competing *identities*, and that my capacity to access competing discourses depends upon my interpretation of myself and my identities in terms of those discourses, and that this in turn depends upon my *identifications* with alternative defining communities.

This process will, of course, involve *disidentifications:* often it is the experience of *not* belonging to a group to which one is assigned that opens up questions of who I am and who I want to be. And this is particularly the case when the social category to which one is assigned is a subordinate, repudiated, or abjected identity. Judith Butler describes disidentification as the "experience of *misrecognition*, this uneasy sense of standing under a sign to which one does and does not belong" (Butler 1993, 219). Drawing on Butler, José Medina argues that the destabilization and resignifications produced by disidentification open up possibilities for transformation: "disidentification can transform the articulation of an identity category and the community organized around it" (Medina 2003, 665). I am arguing that this process involves not just identification and disidentification with a category. It involves alternative identifications with alternative defining communities that open up different meanings and practices, different values and interpretations, and thus different possibilities for identities. This doesn't mean that we ever feel that we completely belong anywhere, and we will inevitably be pulled in different directions by different meanings and different defining communities. And it doesn't mean that any defining community is comfortable or homogeneous: in chapters 2 and 3 I discuss the necessarily heterogeneous and conflictual nature of defining communities. The point is that alternative communities— even if we find them only in books or on television—provide alternative possibilities for identification.[4]

Thus, Taylor is right that the questions that we ask in the quest for authenticity work to undermine ascriptions to oppressive identity categories and lead toward freedom. Because I can understand and criticize the ways in which I am socially constituted in terms of fixed identities only by asking the ethical questions "who am I really?," "who do I really want to be?," and "what really matters to me?," and only through a commitment to an authentic relation to myself (even if these questions and this commitment are not always conscious or explicit.) Of course, we can go some way toward understanding and criticizing social construction and social hierarchy by focusing on objective questions of power, of social justice, and constructions of identity categories. But we won't learn about our own positions in these social relations until we ask questions about ourselves—who am I really? This question requires a Foucaultian answer: an understanding of the ways in which my identity is constituted through regimes of power. But it also requires that we ask ethical questions: what matters to me? Where do I stand? And if we want to understand more clearly who we are as individuals we need to ask the question "who are we?" We need to ask which "we"s matter to us, which best interpret us, which are our defining communities. With whom do I identify? We need also to ask how we are recognized and misrecognized by and within different communities, in different social contexts.

These different ways of framing the question of identity make it clear that while Foucault and Taylor agree that modern identities are *socially constituted*, they understand this to mean very different things. For Taylor, it means that we are embedded in communities, that we participate in social relations of recognition and misrecognition, and are constituted through background ontologies and relations of meaning. For Foucault, "the history which bears and determines us has the form of a war rather than that of a language: relations of power, not relations of meaning" (1980a, 114). For Foucault, we are constituted through "dividing practices" through which we are classified and assigned to social categories (2000, 327). For Taylor, we are constituted through our attachments to "defining communities"—through our identifications with particular traditions, nations, or groups, or moral or political or spiritual commitments. We are constituted through webs of power for Foucault, and through "webs of interlocution" for Taylor. For Foucault we are required to judge ourselves in terms of normalizing code moralities; for Taylor we must define ourselves through our relation to the good, or goods, of our social world. Both, it seems to me, are right. But the different stories have very different implications: for Foucault, the modern social world is a realm of imposition and constraint, and the individual is essentially subjected; as Foucault acknowledges, there is little room for agency in his earlier genealogies. For Taylor, the social is a source of individual freedom: there is no I without a we. The I, or first person singular, is constituted by the we, or first person plural.[5] For Foucault the social is not a "we"; the individual is constituted by the third person of society, which enables us as subjects—as subjected—to conform to or resist third-person social categories. (I shall discuss the role of the social in Foucault's late work in the next section.)

Most importantly, for Taylor, the question, "Who am I?" is not about social category, because what it's really asking is "To what, and to whom, am I importantly *connected*?" This is not a question of my identity *as* something, but a question of my identification and connection *with* and *to* particular people, communities, and ideals. And these questions take us out of the opposition between first and third person, because we are no longer talking about the ways that third-person social categories (categories imposed on us by the social; by *them*) define us. We are talking about the ways that I (first-person singular) am essentially connected with a *we* (first person plural). We might also say that we are talking about the ways that I am connected to *you*: to a "you" that is not a "second person," because it precedes me and gives me my life and my meaning.[6] The "you" is my addressee: those to whom I am addressing, and defining, myself. Thus, freedom from social categories requires freedom through identifications. Freedom is always through but also *to* or *toward* a community or a place where I belong.

The strength of Taylor's approach is his understanding that we are ourselves only through our connections: to others, to goods, to ourselves. To a we and a you. Our identities are not just the effects of our constitution through power regimes; our identities are our connections. We are *participants* in the construction of our own identities, and we participate through interaction and dialogue with others and with ourselves, and through engagement with questions about ourselves and our relationships. But to get to the alternative interpretations of the "single black woman on welfare" we have had to move beyond Taylor. Taylor's valuation of community and our embeddedness in it tends to be conservative, and he tends too often to see social influences as benign. He pays too little attention to the degree to which we still are very much fixed in hierarchical social positions defined by categories like race, class, gender, and sexuality, and still are very much fixed by ascriptions of identity categories. Our construction in terms of these categories and social positions *is*, to a large extent, an effect of modern power. So a Foucaultian analysis is crucial here.[7] For Taylor, the question "who am I?" is primarily a question about the values, goods, commitments and attachments that I affirm. Thus, for example, I can recognize myself as a "householder, father of a family, holding down a job, providing for my dependants; all this can be the basis of my sense of dignity. Just as its absence can be catastrophic, can shatter it by totally undermining my feeling of self-worth" (Taylor, 1989, 15-16). Taylor presents this as an example of how the "affirmation of ordinary life," a specifically modern good, is essential to the householder's identity, and hence to a meaningful life. But he does not go on to argue that the man who derives his dignity from his self-definition as a householder, as the head of a family, cannot really know himself until he recognizes how that self-definition constitutes his dignity *against* the indignity of the single black woman on welfare, or the gay man without family ties. This is not just a question of multiple, different goods, or even a recognition that goods can be in conflict. Taylor discusses both of these problems at length in *Sources of the Self.* Introducing a Foucaultian interpretation requires a recognition that my pride in being the household head *depends* upon the derogation of the "dependent," non-job-holding, non-married, or non-heterosexual other. So that I don't really know who I am until I recognize my privilege as a heterosexual, white, father, and until I recognize how that privilege depends on the subordination of various other classes of people. It is not enough, then, to know what I choose to affirm, or how I am connected to the communities that matter to me. We need to question our defining communities, to consider the ways they are constituted and the ways they constitute us, and we need to analyze the meanings of the social identities that have so far been opaque to us. And this will require new identifications with critical communities.

I want to argue, then, that, following Taylor, and contra Foucault, we need to continue the quest for authenticity if we are to undermine our social ascriptions. We need to ask the ethical questions "who am I?" and "what matters to me?"—we need to keep struggling to get closer to the "truth" of who we are—if we want to pursue the possibility of *freedom* from fixed identities. But, contra Taylor, we can't get very far with this pursuit unless we incorporate Foucault's critique of our constitution through relations of power. Moreover, considering whom one is in relation to various "we"s means we have to go beyond both Taylor and Foucault, while incorporating their insights. For we can't simply accept our collective identities as given, but we also can't assume that collective identities are always fixed and normalizing categories. Resistant identities are often the *result* of a recognition and critique of oppression, and these identities often emerge out of solidarity, out of a desire for association and relationship, rather than the other way around. And we have to go beyond both Taylor and Foucault for understandings of power and freedom developed in feminist theory, critical race theory, queer theory, and postcolonial theories, and to develop understandings of identity in terms of critical relations with defining communities. Here, the work of theorists of positionality and of postpositivist realist theories of identity is essential. Linda Alcoff (1988, 2006), Satya P. Mohanty (1993, 1997), and Paula Moya (2000b, 2002) argue that we need to understand particular identities as constituted by our concrete and historical social positions or locations, and by our interpretations of those positions. Our positions in social and historical contexts "can be actively utilized...as a location for the construction of meaning, a place from where meaning can be *discovered*" (Alcoff 2006, 148). And Moya argues that the alternative interpretations produced through oppositional struggles are fundamental to our ability to understand the world (Moya 2000b, 86).

> In the case of social phenomena like sexism and racism, whose distorted representation benefits the powerful and the established groups and institutions, an attempt at an objective explanation is necessarily continuous with oppositional political struggles. Objective knowledge of such social phenomena is in fact often dependent on the theoretical knowledge that activism creates. For without these alternative constructions and accounts our capacity to interpret and understand the dominant ideologies and institutions is limited to those created or sanctioned by these very ideologies and institutions. (S.P. Mohanty 1997, 213)

In other words, the authenticity question—the question "who am I?," which is essential for an authentic relation to self—has to be answered complexly, through analyses of my objective positions in power relations, through subjective ethical questions about what matters to me, and through practical identifications with communities of critique and resistance, as well as with communities of origin. And this process does not end. We need to be able to criticize all of our defining communities, those we find ourselves in and those we find for ourselves. This does not mean that we necessarily reject or escape them, but that we renegotiate our connections, find different ways of connecting and identifying.[8] We need to do this in order to get past the false individualism of modern culture, to discover and develop our identities and our freedom as fully social beings.

I am making the strong claim that to the extent that my important social and political identities are not salient to me, to the extent that I fail adequately to examine what these mean, to that extent I will *fail* to recognize the social and historical *truth* of myself and my relations to others, and I will *fail* to progress toward freedom from fixed identities. This means that if we think our identities are just about what is salient for me, what I *choose* to identify with, then we are failing to understand who we really are. The fact that we are constituted through social contexts and through regimes of power means that we don't know ourselves until we understand those contexts and those power regimes.[9]

This does not mean, of course, that we can ever discover and know any final truth about ourselves: again, the conception of truth I am employing here is concrete, social, and historical. It does mean that the recognition that we are socially and historically constituted does not, as Foucault sometimes claims it does, obviate the necessity or the possibility of self-knowledge. In response to a question as to how his view differs from Sartrean existentialism, Foucault answers:

> I think that from the theoretical point of view, Sartre avoids the idea of the self as something which is given to us, but through the moral notion of authenticity, he turns back to the idea that we have to be ourselves—to be truly our true self. I think that the only acceptable practical consequence of what Sartre has said is to link his theoretical insight to the practice of creativity—and not of authenticity. From the idea that the self is not given to us, I think that there is only one practical consequence: we have to create ourselves as a work of art. (1984b, 351)

Foucault's argument for a shift to a practice of self-creation is important. But in opposing self-creation against a "true self" he is falling back on a false dichotomy between a self that is given and a self that is to be created. What does it mean to have an authentic relation to self—to try to discover the truth of oneself—when the self is historically and socially constituted? It means, in part, including Foucaultian genealogical analysis in the answer: developing a better understanding of the historical, social, political "truth" of who we are. Foucault's genealogies actually enjoin us to reflect on this kind of historically and socially produced truth. But the fact that the self is not given but is socially and historically constituted also means that we are participants in our own self-constitution; and the practice of self-creation requires that we ask questions about what and who matter to us. Our practices of self-creation both presuppose and create new connections, new identifications; and as our connections change so do our truths. For Foucault, the imperative to be truly ourselves needs to be rejected, and replaced with the ideal of self-creation. "Maybe the target nowadays is not to discover who we are but to refuse what we are" (2000, 336). I would argue that being truly oneself does not mean accessing some pre-given core of self; it means participating fully and critically in one's connections. This requires that we continually ask questions about our most important identifications, and that through those questions we shift, renegotiate, transform, and affirm our identifications. The sustained critique of given truths, the testing of limits and the acts of self-creation that Foucault affirms in "What is Enlightenment?" are not possible without access to and creation of alternative defining communities and ideals to which we are strongly connected, with which we are strongly identified.

Self-Creation and Meaning: Freedom as a Practice of Belonging

I have been focusing on the question of freedom and its relation to truth; in particular, to the truth of oneself. I have been arguing that freedom requires self-knowledge. But the dialogue at the beginning of this chapter, the dialogue between Samad and Irie, is not primarily about—although it is partly about—knowing who you are. Samad's focus is on what gives his life *meaning*. As I have noted, the question of *authenticity* is not just about knowing the truth of the self; it's about being true *to* oneself. And this relation to self is an ethical relation, because it focuses on the question of a *meaningful life*. For Taylor, the question of what gives my life meaning is the central question of identity. For Samad, there can be no meaning without belonging.

Irie, on the other hand, is looking not for meaning but for freedom. We could say that she is looking for the freedom to create herself without entanglement in webs of belonging. For Foucault, freedom requires not only the permanent critique of given truths, but the capacity to engage in the project of self-creation, self-invention, without enforced conformity to normalizing code moralities and the identities they prescribe.

How do we balance the quest for a meaningful life with the quest for freedom? Both Taylor and the late Foucault try to do this with their accounts of creative and social selves.

For Taylor, our lives have meaning only insofar as we experience ourselves as importantly *connected*: to our defining communities, to our background horizons, to our ideals and goods. As Samad Iqbal puts it, without this sense of connection, of belonging, how can we feel that anything matters at all? So, for Taylor, we need to ask the authenticity question not only to free ourselves from fixed identities, but also to discover and create and affirm our connections. This is a communitarian ideal, and it can be a conservative one: it can focus on a tradition, on preserving a past. But the focus on connection can also be an orientation to a future: to alternative, resistant identities, to the creation of new defining communities, to an ideal future, a better, more meaningful life, in a better world.

Surely Taylor is right that a meaningful life does involve connection. As Samad makes clear, the question of a meaningful life does not arise until we are disconnected, dislocated—until we have become "free" from connections that have held us together. This kind of freedom is the freedom of alienation: disconnection. A life without meaning is a life in which one is not importantly connected to anything, or anyone. And being connected means *identifying* oneself *with*: with a past or tradition, with defining communities, with values or ideals, with a future one can imagine or foresee.

From the perspective of the early Foucault, we can argue that a meaningful life can be a life of subjection. The fact that I affirm particular goods, that I identify myself within particular defining communities, and experience myself as belonging, can mean just that I have been thoroughly subjected. The meaning or mattering that, for Taylor, enables us to be ourselves, enables us only to be ourselves in subjection to social norms, for Foucault. And what does it mean to say that my meanings are mine, if I am not the author of these meanings? Why should I affirm them? Taylor argues that we need to resist the attitude of suspicion toward our own meanings and identities. We need to have *faith* in our connections, our meanings, our identities, as real goods. In *Sources of the Self,* Taylor argues that we can defend the "reality" of our values and meanings, against naturalist arguments that values are just projections of some physical state and against Nietzschean and Foucaultian arguments that our meanings are just expressions of power, with recourse to what he calls the "best account" principle (Taylor, 1989, 58–9, 99–103). A belief in the reality of our values and meanings is warranted, Taylor argues, because they make the best sense of our lives. In other words, he is arguing that we can defend a *participant* understanding against a purely *observer* understanding of our values and meanings. We can't live our lives according to a Nietzschean ironization of our own values, meanings, connections, identities. With Taylor, I would argue that we affirm our meanings as goods, because they make the best sense of lives. And that we can support them with reasons—not because they are "rational" but because they are essential to our relationships. We have what I would call *affective reasons* for embracing them: because they connect me to my significant others, to my projects, to my self.

But what if the participant—Irie, for example—does not experience any connections as essential to her life? What if identities and their connections are experienced as external, imposed, produced, or contingent to oneself? What if identities can be lived only ironically, as fictions? Well, Taylor and Samad would argue that such a life is an alienated life, a life without meaning. Unless Irie can embrace some connections, her life will be an empty one. But isn't that the point? That we moderns are all alienated, that we can live our identities only ironically because we can't really have faith in them? Is the answer simply to exhort us to have faith? On the other hand, few of us are entirely without connections that we can affirm or identities that have meaning for us. Most of us are more like the example of the "single black woman on welfare" who is struggling to negotiate her identity. And like her, we waver among competing meanings. Do I want to be independent? Or are the resistant interpretations right? Which identifications are the strongest and most meaningful for me? What do "black" and "woman" mean for me? With whom do I want to align myself? Does it matter where I came from, who I belong to, what I care about, or is it just an accident? Sometimes she does experience herself as dependent, does identify most strongly with the community of those (including many of her black friends and family) who believe that she is a drain on society until she gets a job. Sometimes, by identifying with resistant communities, she experiences herself as a strong and resistant and good woman and mother. We could say that she is struggling to live between the two frames of faith and suspicion. Between faith in defining identities and the unmasking of their forms of oppression. The problem becomes, then, how to live between the two frames: between faith and unmasking. One way to respond to this problem is to oscillate back and forth between identity and non-identity: faith and suspicion; belonging and freedom. But there is another way to interpret and respond to the problem. We could say that we are negotiating among multiple and conflicting identifications. And finding new ways to hold these together, through recreating and redefining our identities, renegotiating and recreating our attachments. To do this, we need to recognize that our goods are generally going to be what I would call "mixed goods": there will be aspects of them that we find oppressive and cannot endorse. For example, one's identities as a woman, as a mother, as a wage-earner, as a member of a particular ethnic group, as queer, may be goods that give life meaning, and they may also be sources of constraint and oppression. But we will not find our freedom only by unmasking them as oppressive, and we cannot always—and often do not wish to—escape or subvert them; we will have to find—to create—ways of transforming them, of living them differently.

In his late work on the ethics of the self, Foucault began to look for an alternative, or supplement, to the hermeneutics of suspicion, to shift from the analysis of the subject from an observer perspective to an understanding of the self as an agent who is a participant in a social world. We could say that Foucault's late work is about the possibility of faith: faith in the future, in the possibility of self-creation. It's also about connection: to a telos or ideal of a life of creative practice and innovation, of life as a work of art. We could say that Foucault's late work is an attempt to conceptualize a self that can affirm its relations, its identifications. Recognizing that his early work lacked a conception of agency, of the self as participant in one's own life, Foucault draws on the Greeks for a model of an ethics, and an ethical relation to self, in which the mode of subjection is aesthetic rather than normative, the ethical substance is actions or practices rather than identity, the techne or askesis is work on the self, and the telos is the beautiful life, life as a work of art (1984b). This is a model of freedom grounded not just in escape from constraints (negative freedom) but in relation to oneself and one's telos. We could also say that for Foucault the free creation of the self, of the beautiful life, is what gives life meaning—is what makes for a meaningful life. This is why the ethical relation to self is ethical. And it is the connection to or identification with the ideal of self-creation that makes it meaningful. Conversely, we can also say that it is this connection that constitutes freedom. Real freedom would be a life in which one is deeply connected: a meaningful life.

For Foucault, this kind of relation to self is very different from modern identity. If Foucault affirms faith in self-creation, he remains consistently suspicious of identities. But as we have seen, for Taylor this relation to self and to one's telos *is* one's identity—or is an essential part of one's identity. In *Sources of the Self* Taylor argues that the beautiful life may be one telos among many possible goods recognized by modern western subjects. He identifies several such goods, and we can surely identify many more, especially once we broaden our global horizons. Taylor also recognizes that modern subjects generally embrace several competing and conflicting goods—but he suggests that by developing our capacities for articulating our goods, by articulating them more carefully and clearly, we might be able to reconcile some of these conflicts.

For Taylor, however, the connection to an ideal self, without any account of connection to defining communities, or histories, is a rather thin connection. By itself, an orientation to a future of my own creation is difficult to distinguish from liberal atomism.

Unless one can experience meaningful connectedness not only to the future selves one *chooses* (or creates or invents) but also to the others, the "we"s that precede and expand oneself, then according to Taylor and Samad, one is living an alienated life. Without an experience of belonging to defining communities—without an experience of these as more than just external conditions, regimes that produce us—then we are atomistic individuals. If my meaning and my freedom consist only in my self-invention, with no expansion of myself beyond the line between me and my future self, with no connections laterally, or backward, with no ability to discover and find meaning in those connections that I have *not chosen,* then I will fail to live a meaningful life. My freedom, then, must be social freedom: must be situated in my social connections.

Foucault's ethics of the self does tend to slide into liberal atomism. "If we are asked to relate to the question of identity, it must be an identity to our unique selves. And the relationships we have to have with ourselves are not ones of identity. To be the same is really boring. Identity...is useful, but it limits us, and we have a right to be free" (1997b, 166). This attitude is not atypical of Foucault's work on the self and its freedom. In general, Foucault equates shared identities with boring and oppressive sameness, rather than with connections to other people. He also still tends to equate sociality with systematization and argues for an ethics unrelated to any social institutions; he notes approvingly that for the ancient Greeks "ethics was not related to any social—or at least to any legal—institutional system" (1984b, 343).

In a few places, Foucault does, however, attempt to situate his model of the ethical relation to self in social relations. The Greeks, after all, believed themselves to be essentially social beings.[10] In the ethics of the self that Foucault attributes to the Greeks, the self is a social self insofar as he (and he is very much a he) fulfils social roles, lives with and governs others, and learns from others. More importantly, the mode of subjection, the ethical substance, the techne or askesis, and the telos are all socially defined: the implication is that we should not be suspicious of social roles, practices, and definitions simply because they are social, or shared in common. "[I]f I am now interested in how the subject constitutes itself in an active fashion through practices of the self, these practices are nevertheless not something invented by the individual himself. They are models that he finds in his culture and are proposed, suggested, imposed upon him by his culture, his society, and his social group" (1997a, 291). Foucault argues that the aesthetic relation to self is far better than the modern normalizing code morality as a means to sustaining social relations.

But Foucault's understanding of relations with others, and of the social self, is rather undeveloped.[11] He does attempt, in response to questioning, to note the importance of "care for others" in the model of the care of the self that he takes from the Greeks. (He stresses, however, that "what makes it ethical for the Greeks is not that it is care for others. The care of the self is ethical in itself" (1997a, 287).) But his examples of the ways in which care for self is also care for others fall considerably short of any recognizable criteria for what might constitute care for others. For the Greeks, Foucault argues, "this *ethos* of freedom is also a way of caring for others. This is why it is important for a free man who conducts himself as he should to be able to govern his wife, his children, his household; it is also the art of governing." Secondly, "the care of the self enables one to occupy his rightful position in the city, the community, or interpersonal relationships, whether as a magistrate or a friend." Thirdly, "the care of the self also implies a relationship with the other insofar as proper care of the self requires listening to the lessons of a master" (1997a, 287). But the head of the household who "governs" his wife and children, who fulfils social roles as he should, and who learns from a teacher or guide, is hardly a model of "caring for others."[12]

Foucault's claim that the early Romans' practices of care for self constituted a "true social practice" is no more convincing. For Foucault, this activity devoted to oneself constituted a "true social practice" because it took form within more or less "institutionalized structures," because it involved "speaking and writing…and communicating with others," and because it was supported by "customary relations of kinship, friendship and obligation. When, in the practice of the care of the self, one appealed to another person in whom one recognized an aptitude for guidance and counselling, one was exercising a right…. The care of the self appears therefore as intrinsically linked to a 'soul service,' which includes the possibility of a round of exchanges with the other and a system of reciprocal obligations" (1986, 51–4). These passages only underline the fact that the social, for Foucault, is a sphere of institution-alized structures rather than social connections, and of liberal exchanges of rights and obligations rather than any significant interdependence. Nor does the role of the *hypomnemata,* the journals in which the words of others are recorded, as part of the practice of the care of the self, provide evidence that the practice of the care of the self is a "true social practice" (1984b, 364).

There is much more to the social self than the fact that we interact with others and fulfil social roles. Liberal theories recognize these facts as well. What's missing, of course, is the depth: for Taylor, and for Samad, our social-ity is defined by a deep subjective experience of belonging, an experience that gives life meaning, that makes life worth living. For modern western subjects, the significance of this experience is provoked by an existential question—by the experience, or the possibility, of alienation, dislocation. And for Taylor, our sociality is defined also by an ontology of the self in which the self is essentially connected and interdependent: we could not *be* ourselves without significant attachments, defining communities, for we are continually consti-tuted through engagement in relations of dialogue and recognition.

It is fair to say that this strong conception of the social self was an absence throughout Foucault's work. To be more precise, he gave us a brilliant analysis of our sociality insofar as we are produced through modern social regimes of power, but he was unable to conceive of a self that is social insofar as its social-ity provides its meaning.

Foucault might have developed a better understanding of the social self in the work that he was beginning before he died. He does ask, but does not fol-low up on, the question as to whether we could have "an ethics of acts and their pleasures which would be able to take into account the pleasure of the other" (1984b, 346). In some late interviews, Foucault suggested that he wanted to study the history of friendship: with the development of modernity, he argued, close friendships began to be perceived as dangerous, because modern disciplinary institutions could not operate in the face of intense friendships, especially friendships among men. Modern homophobia, Foucault suggests, developed not so much out of an abhorrence of sexual acts but because of the potential for affectional relations outside the normative patterns, and the danger that such relations would disrupt those patterns (1997b, 170–71). It is impossible, of course, to know just where this research might have led Foucault.

In the body of work that Foucault did produce, social relations are typi-cally understood as power relations. In "What is Enlightenment?" Foucault described his life's project as the study of our "practical systems" in three broad domains, organized along three axes: relations of control over things (knowledge), relations of action upon others (power), and relations with oneself (ethics) (1984a, 48). It is significant that there is no place, in this schema, for relations *with* others: Foucault replaces Kantian morality, which focused precisely on the problem of relations with others, with a model in which relations between subjects could be understood only as power relations, and in which the only relation *with* anyone, or anything, is the relation with oneself. I have already argued for a conception of knowledge of oneself that is very different from any conception of knowledge as control over things.

In fact, the inadequacy of modern code moralities is one point on which Foucault and Taylor agree. Both are critical of modern code moralities, but for opposing reasons. Foucault argues that modern code morality focused on universally applicable rights and obligations works through the normalizing production of identities through practices of interrogation and self-interrogation to determine whether one is conforming to the norm. Thus, he argues for a move out of our focus on identity into doing, into innovative practices. Taylor argues that modern code moralities focus too narrowly on doing, on procedures for action, and leave out our identities—our values and goods, our attachments and commitments—leave out, in short, the sources of the sense and meaning of our actions. Again, this opposition is an effect of their opposing understandings of what identity is. Both Taylor and Foucault are criticizing the way in which code moralities render us docile machines, doing what is right by following rules that are given to us, that are produced and enforced through relations of power, without any motivation or positive relation to right action that might be said to be one's own. Both argue for an ethics in which one does what is right because one is motivated by the desire to care for, attend to, or be true to oneself: to one's telos, or values. For Taylor, as we have seen, the capacity to identify one's telos, or goods, is what defines one's identity. My identity is defined by that with which I most strongly *identify*. Foucault does not want to call this self-relation an *identity*; for Foucault identity can be only a fixed truth that precludes innovation. Foucault does, however, say this: "Ethics is the considered form that freedom takes when it is informed by reflection" (1997a, 284). Ethics, in other words, is defined in terms of the actions of free and self-reflective agents: agents who govern themselves according to reflection on what kind of selves they want to be, a question that turns on recognizing who and what they identify with. For Foucault, this necessarily involves innovation. For Taylor, this necessarily involves recognizing our attachment to defining communities.

Yet, there is a sense in which both Taylor's and Foucault's ethics are oddly *asocial.* Neither Taylor nor Foucault adequately thematizes the central importance, for any ethics, of a relation to a universal or concrete other as an end. In focusing their ethics on the relation to self, they focus on *my* relation to my own values or ideals. An ethics, however, cannot be all about me. An ethics needs, as Foucault and Taylor both recognize, to be about how to be with others. But in focusing their ethics—their accounts of motivation for sustaining social relationships—on my relation to my goods, they shift the focus from the other to the self. Both do this to provide an alternative to moral codes focused exclusively on universal norms. But in rejecting moral codes they also reject an ethics oriented toward the other—a *you*—as an end. I would argue that an alternative ethics needs to include my relation to my goods, but needs also to include, importantly, my relation to you as an end, both universal and concrete. This is not just a question of morality, narrowly construed. A free and meaningful life needs to incorporate reflective relations to others, not just as objects of my social roles, and not just as my defining communities, but as ends in themselves.

I have argued, then, that practices of freedom, including struggles for freedom from fixed identities and the regimes of power that produce them, require struggles for self-knowledge, and that these entail identifications with alternative and resistant defining communities, which offer alternative and resistant identities. Once we understand identities as not only effects of power but as our connections to others, and to what matters to us, it is possible to see identities as not only effects of subjection but as sources of liberation. And the sustained critique of given truths, the testing of limits and the acts of self-creation that Foucault affirms in "What is Enlightenment?" are not possible without access to and creation of alternative defining communities. Freedom, then, is an ongoing practice of finding and creating and affirming as well as questioning and criticizing our identities, which are our connections. Once practices of freedom are understood to be renegotiations of our connections, then practices of freedom can be compatible with the practice of a meaningful life lived with others: a practice of interdependence, or social freedom. Finally, I have suggested that an ethics of the self needs to focus on not just my freedom or on what matters to me but on others, and on my relations to others, as ends. I have argued, then, that by combining and moving beyond Taylor and Foucault it becomes possible to understand struggles for self-knowledge and for meaning—struggles for identity—as practices of freedom, which involve critical and transformative identifications with defining communities and critical and transformative relations with others.

In the next chapter, I shall take up feminist debates on the themes of identity, freedom, and the idea of "home." Drawing on the arguments made in this chapter, I shall argue that rather than oscillating between identity and nonidentity, faith and suspicion, belonging and freedom, it is possible to develop both individual critical identities and transformed identity politics through negotiating multiple and conflicting identifications. This depends on understanding identities and homes as sites for the risk of connection, rather than withdrawal into privacy and safety. For individuals, this involves, again, engaging in a process of self-creation that includes a pursuit of self-knowledge, reflecting on the relations of power that constitute us, but that is motivated and sustained by relations of love and solidarity. This opens up a conception of freedom in relation to a transformed ideal of "home" as a place where we can risk and sustain relationship through conflict. And it opens up a conception of identity politics as a politics of solidarity rooted in this transformed ideal of "home."

Notes

1. See Ricoeur (1970) 28–36, for a discussion of these two traditions. See also Descombes (1982) for a discussion of the reception of the two traditions in France.
2. Diana Meyers (2004) develops a strong argument for an ideal of authenticity that is compatible with intersectional identities. Meyers addresses critiques of the concept of authenticity, criticizes the conception of authenticity in Frankfurt (1988), and develops an analysis of the competencies required for members of subordinated groups to develop autonomy and authenticity. See also Meyers (1989).
3. It should be clear that the conceptions of "truth" I am employing here are not any kind of essential or absolute Truth, but are conceptions consistent with our finitude, locatedness, and historicity as selves in process. The first conception is ethical: When I ask the ethical question, "what do I care about?" my answers will depend on the context and location of the question, and are interpretations of my values and commitments. The second conception is explicitly social and historical: what are the relations of power through which I have been constituted?
4. And while they do get mixed up in practice, it is important to distinguish conceptually between identity categories and ethical commitments: disidentification from identity categories is one thing; disidentification from your own values and commitments is another thing altogether. For an insightful discussion of disidentification from one's own commitments, see Cheshire

Calhoun (2008).Of course it is also the case that we are often divided and ambivalent about our identifications.I continue the discussion of disidentification in chapter 3.

5. The understanding of the "we" as first-person plural, in contrast to the assumption that any "we" is necessarily opposed to a "them" or a "you," is developed by Habermas. "The expression 'we' is used not only in collective speech actions vis-à-vis an addressee who assumes the communicative role of *you*, under the reciprocity condition that *we* in turn are *you* for them. In individual speech actions, *we* can also be used in such a way that a corresponding sentence presupposes not the complementary relation to another group but that to other individuals of one's own group" (Habermas 1979,107–8). This understanding of the "we" is developed by Jodi Dean (1996). Habermas's understanding of the "we" is informed by his reading of G.H. Mead. For a discussion of Mead's conception of the generalized other in relation to the "we" of identity see José Medina (2006). See also Weir (1995).

6. Lorraine Code (1995) and Annette Baier (1997) both argue that the second-person perspective precedes the first-person. See also Adriana Cavarero (2000).

7. Here I am not arguing that Foucault explicitly focuses on these particular identities. Neither Taylor nor Foucault does that. I am arguing that a Foucaultian analysis of our constitution in terms of identity categories is essential to our understanding of our constitution in terms of these particular categories.

8. In some cases, of course, we can escape; but many of our identities and defining communities are inescapable: we can't simply choose *not* to be black, or a woman, or transgendered, or from our family of origin.

9. This point is also made by Paula Moya, drawing on Satya P. Mohanty. Identities, Moya argues, are "evaluatable theoretical claims that have epistemic consequences. Who we understand ourselves to be will have consequences for how we experience and understand the world. Our conceptions of who we are as social beings (our identities) influence—and in turn are influenced by—our understandings of how our society is structured and what our particular experiences in that society are likely to be. The point, however, is that our different views about how our society is structured and where we and others fit into that totality are not all equally accurate.... Identities are thus not simply products of structures of power; they are often assumed or chosen for complex subjective reasons that can be objectively evaluated (Moya 2000a, 9).

10. Foucault argues that, contrary to Hegelian wisdom, the Greeks did have a conception of individual freedom: freedom for the Greeks consisted in the capacity for self-mastery, in not being a slave, in ascribing to an ethics as the conscious practice of freedom, or care or the self (1997a, 285). This is clearly very different from modern western conceptions of individual freedom based on ownership of private property, rights, and negative freedom from the public realm.

But in Foucault's account we do find a conception of freedom similar to the capacity for self-realization and expression which Taylor identifies as definitively modern.

11. For discussions of this point see Allen (2004), McLaren (1997), Grimshaw (1993), McNay (1992), Sawicki (1991), Dews (1989), and Balbus (1987).

12. On this point see Allen (2004) and McLaren (1997).

2 HOME AND IDENTITY

IN MEMORY OF IRIS MARION YOUNG

I think how I just want to feel at home, where people know me; instead I remember…that home was a place of forced subservience, and I know that my wish is that of an adult wanting to stay a child; to be known by others, but to know nothing, to feel no responsibility.

The place that I missed sometimes seemed like a memory of childhood, but it was not a childish place. It was a place of mutuality, companionship, creativity, sensuousness, easiness in the body, curiosity…hope…safety and love.

MINNIE BRUCE PRATT

In this chapter, I want to revisit some feminist reflections on home, and particularly on home as a metaphor for identity. In the late 1980s and early 1990s, several feminist theorists, drawing on Minnie Bruce Pratt's "Identity: Skin Blood Heart," used the metaphor of home to identify the problematic and illusory nature of an ideal of individual identity as bounded, unified, safe and secure, and an ideal of a feminist politics emerging out of a cohesive community of women-identified women. It was recognized that these safe and secure homes were in fact founded on repressions and exclusions, on defenses and on the policing of borders. This recognition marked a decisive break from the white middle-class feminist politics of Virginia Woolf's 1928 classic *A Room of One's Own*. As Bernice Johnson Reagon put it, once you let all the strangers in, "the room don't feel like a room no more. And it ain't home no more" (1983, 346). And, as Teresa de Lauretis argued, the home was never really home in the first place; women have never been at home. De Lauretis urged us to embrace and affirm our displacement from home, as "eccentric subjects" (1990).

In her 1997 essay, "House and Home: Feminist Variations on a Theme," Iris Marion Young argues that while the ideal of home and women's association with home have been and are in many ways oppressive to women, there are aspects of the ideal of home that we ought to reclaim. Young argues that "while politics should not succumb to a longing for comfort and unity, the material values of home can nevertheless provide leverage for radical social critique" (157).[1] Thus, Young is arguing that the ideal of home ought to be affirmed as a locus of goods—normative values—that support personal and collective identity, and that should be accessible to everyone. They stand, Young argues, as "regulative ideals by which societies should be criticized" (161). These values are: 1) safety, 2) individuation, 3) privacy, and 4) preservation.

The feminist theorists Young is addressing—Biddy Martin and Chandra Mohanty (1986), Teresa de Lauretis (1990), and Bonnie Honig (1994)—have all argued that just these values should be criticized, or rejected: the ideal of safety should be replaced with an openness to risk and danger, the ideal of individuation with an acceptance of a nonunified self, the ideal of privacy with a critique of the public-private split, and the ideal of preservation with an orientation toward the future and toward change. I shall argue, first of all, that while the critiques of home are important, Young's defenses remind us that home and identity are, in her words, "critical values" that should indeed be accessible to all. But I shall also argue that we need to move beyond both critiques and defenses of home to criticize the dichotomies themselves: that home can also be understood as a locus of values that transcend dichotomies. These values are: 1) the risk of connection, and of sustaining relationship through conflict; 2) relational identities, constituted through both relations of power, and relations of mutuality, love, and flourishing; 3) relational autonomy: freedom as the capacity to be in relationships one desires, and freedom as expansion of self in relationship; 4) connection to past and future, through reinterpretive preservation and transformative identification.

From Safety vs. Risk to the Risk of Connection

"Identity: Skin Blood Heart" is a classic feminist analysis of identity through the metaphor of home. Pratt's narrative is an account of her own movement through a series of identities, and her deconstruction of those identities. At each stage, she analyzes the construction of her own identity through relations of power and exclusion, through racism, sexism, homophobia, and class hierarchies, and she uncovers layer upon layer of lies, fear, oppression, denial, struggle, and resistance within each of her comfortable homes. For Pratt, the very desire for home, for comfort, safety, and protection, is suspect. She comes to realize that her safety and protection have been bought at a price: as a white southern Christian female, she has been protected from black men and Jews, kept pure for childbearing; the home she grew up in was stolen from indigenous peoples and built through the labor of slaves. And she learns that her safety is conditional. When she falls in love with a woman, she steps outside the circle of protection that kept her safe as a white heterosexual wife and mother. Her children are taken away from her. The ideal of home as a place of safety and protection has been exposed as a lie, a romantic illusion whose seductive pull she must resist. This story is repeated each time she finds a new identity, a new home. When she finds a home as a woman-identified woman, she has to learn, slowly and painfully, how that home too is built on the exclusion of women unlike herself: nonwhite, non-Christian, not middle class. Pratt learns to live a life that is less comfortable and less safe but more truthful and less lonely: "I will try to be at the edge between my fear and outside, on the edge at my skin, listening, asking what new thing will I hear, will I see, will I let myself feel, beyond the fear" (1988, 18).

In their thoughtful analysis of Pratt's text, Biddy Martin and Chandra Mohanty write that Pratt's descriptions of each of the places she's lived, and each of her identities in those places, are constructed on a tension between two modalities: home and not home. "'Being home' refers to the place where one lives within familiar, safe, protected boundaries; 'not being home' is a matter of realizing that home was an illusion of coherence and safety based on the exclusion of specific histories of oppression and resistance, repression of differences even within oneself" (1986, 196).

Iris Young argues that while Martin and Mohanty are right to point out that the boundaries of home typically serve to protect privilege, they are wrong to reject the ideal of home altogether. For Young, "the proper response is not to reject home, but to extend its positive values to everyone" (159). Young's claim that Martin and Mohanty reject the ideal of home is not quite accurate; their position is more complex. They argue for an acceptance of the "irreconcilable tension between the search for a secure place from which to speak, within which to act, and the awareness of the price at which secure places are bought" (1986, 206). They argue against a purely deconstructive approach, which would negate any identification with one's own historically specific identities, and make a case instead for a situated historical subjectivity. Pratt, they note, "succeeds in carefully taking apart the bases of her own privilege by resituating herself again and again in the social…to reanchor herself repeatedly in each of the positions from which she speaks, even as she works to expose the illusory coherence of those positions" (194). In other words, the position taken by Martin and Mohanty is not that we need to reject the ideal of home altogether, but that we need to live on the tension between home and not home, identity and nonidentity, safety and risk, oscillating back and forth between the two. They do, however, *reduce* the ideal of home to the maintenance of exclusion and oppression. They argue that the safety of home can *only* be bought at the price of exclusion and oppression of others. Thus, even though at the beginning of their essay they stress the importance of "not handing over notions of home and community to the Right" (191), they offer no positive content to an alternative ideal of home. Throughout the essay, they equate home with oppression and exclusion. Thus, while they acknowledge the desire for home, they argue that this desire must be repeatedly undercut by the recognition that the yearned-for safety is illusory, a protection bought at the price of exclusion of others.

The importance of Young's argument, then, is her recognition that the ideal of home should not be reduced to a mechanism of oppression, that "home carries a core positive meaning" that can and should be reclaimed (159). While acknowledging the importance of Luce Irigaray's critique of woman's role as idealized mother/home for man (1992), Young argues that this critique should not persuade us that there is thus no value to the ideal of a safe home. Young notes that bell hooks (1990) agrees that "home" is associated with safety, but she gives a positive and political meaning to these functions of "home." "Appealing to the historic experience of African American women, [hooks] argues that 'homeplace' is the site of resistance to dominating and exploiting social structures. The ability to resist dominant social structures requires a space beyond the full reach of those structures, where different, more humane, social relations can be lived and imagined" (159). Young argues, then, that *safety* is a normative value that should be accessible to all. "Everyone needs a place where they can go to be safe. Ideally, home means a safe place, where one can retreat from the dangers and hassles of collective life" (161).

Surely, Young has a point here. In a world where millions of people are homeless, and millions more are refugees or immigrants whose displacement from home has emphatically not been chosen, the argument that "home" can be understood only as a mechanism of oppression and exclusion can sound vaguely obscene. A safe home is something that, in a just world, would be accessible to everyone. And bell hooks shows how crucial the safety of home can be as a site of protection from and resistance to oppression. Cheshire Calhoun (2000) argues that the *displacement* of lesbians and gays from the safety and protection of the private sphere is central to lesbian and gay subordination; thus full access to that safety and protection is essential to ending lesbian and gay subordination. Young's own argument is partly motivated by her own story, embedded in this essay, of being taken from her home and placed in foster care as a child. Against the background of these forcible displacements from home, the argument that we ought to reject the safety of home and embrace risk and danger appears not as a rejection but as an expression of privilege. Perhaps we could say, then, that the privileged need to question their cozy homes, while the oppressed need to have access to them.

In response to the argument that the prevalence of domestic violence belies the illusion of home as a safe place, Young responds, citing Anita Allen (1988), that, given our awareness that homes are all too often the sites of violence and abuse, the ideal of a safe home serves as a regulative ideal that enables social criticism. It is important, then, to hold onto the possibility, the ideal, of a safety—a home—that is *not* based on exclusion and oppression, that is not a place of violence and abuse, and to maintain that this is essential for a minimally decent life in a minimally just world. This requires that we move beyond cynicism with respect to the possibility of safety: beyond the conviction that reality is inevitably characterized by oppression and exclusion, and that safety is just a nostalgic dream. Young is right, then, to affirm the value of safety, and of home as a safe place.

Yet we need also to move beyond the dichotomy of home/not home, of safety and risk, to imagine an alternative: I want to argue for an ideal of home as a site of the risk of connection, of sustaining relationship through conflict. Thus, rather than oscillating between the desire for a safe, secure, conflict-free home and the recognition that homes are in fact sites of violence and abuse, predicated on oppression and exclusion, we can recognize and affirm an ideal of home as a space of mutuality and conflict, of love and its risks and struggles, of caring and conflictual connections to others. In particular, our political homes—including our identity politics—might be seen as places where we engage in the risk of connection with each other, in the conflictual, messy, dangerous, and intimate work of engagement with each other—engagement in dialogue, in arguments, in struggles, in openness to vulnerability, to critique and self-critique, and to change, with a commitment to solidarity with each other that mediates our commitment to our shared struggles. Shifting to an ideal of home as the space where we risk connection might help us set clear limits on conflict and risk, so that these do not develop into violence. This might enable us to address the violence that is a response to terror and anger at those who threaten our comfort and safety, and the violence that is an assertion of right to dominate the other within the walls of home. If we are not looking for perfect safety, for absolute privacy, for a return to the womb, for the mother who is the angel of the house, perhaps we can learn not to accept violence and oppression as the price of that dream. Perhaps we can imagine and embrace a different dream of a better home.

Thus, rather than rejecting identity politics as a false home, and turning to strategic coalitions of disconnected individuals, we might embrace the possibility of identity politics (and coalition politics?) as homes—as sites of the connections and conflicts essential to solidarity. Surely, Bernice Reagon is right to point out that when we do feminist politics we should not be looking for safety. Coalition politics are necessarily risky and dangerous, and when we are doing this work we can feel ourselves "threatened to the core" (1983, 343). For Reagon, this means that we should not confuse coalition with home: we must separate the two. But if we are able to shift to an ideal of home as a space where we are able to recognize and confront power relations—which surely exist in the safest of homes—and if we are able to sustain relationship through these confrontations, and through the feelings of risk and danger they entail, then we might question the stark opposition between the safety of home and the danger of politics; between home as a place of happy unity and politics as a site of hostile collisions. We might imagine overlapping spheres of homes that are places where we risk connection. This does not mean that everywhere should be home. But shifting to this alternative ideal of home might help us risk connection in our political lives, and it might help us be more realistic about our expectations of home. It might also help those who are privileged to welcome strangers into their homes. And this might help us move closer toward Reagon's ideal of an "old-age perspective" (1983, 348). "The only way you can take yourself seriously is if you can throw yourself into the next period beyond your little meager human-body-mouth-talking all the time.... You must believe that believing in human beings in balance with the environment and the universe is a good thing" (352–53). With these words, Reagon holds out for us the dream of a better home, which we can create only by expanding ourselves to embrace connection. Surely, the only way we can get closer to this dream is by recognizing that our ideal of home must include conflict and struggle.

Individuation: From Identity vs. Nonidentity to Relational Identities

This alternative ideal of home can help us rethink Young's second normative value: Young argues that the ideal of home ought to be affirmed as a support for *individuation*. Where Martin and Mohanty argue for a situated subjectivity constituted through oscillation between identity and nonidentity, home and not home, because, for them, "stable notions of self and identity are based on exclusion and secured by terror" (1986, 197), Young proposes an ideal of home as a space of ownership of material supports for bodily needs and material belongings that reflect one back to oneself, providing a coherence and stability to the self (162). Young is not endorsing the individuation of the independent atomistic individual. She argues for something closer to the kind of process subjectivity that Martin and Mohanty affirm: an "individual subjectivity of the person, where the subject is understood as fluid, partial, shifting," but she adds that this subjectivity exists "in relations of reciprocal support with others" (Young 1997a, 141).

Young and Martin and Mohanty are all arguing for a recognition that our identities are *relational*, but they differ as to what this means. For Young, it means that we are connected to a place where we belong, and to people and belongings that connect us to our selves. For Martin and Mohanty, Pratt's identity is relational primarily because it is constituted through relations of power.[2] Thus Pratt's connections to particular places and people are continually "undermined" and "undercut" by the discovery that they have "obscured particular race, class and gender struggles" (1986, 196). Martin and Mohanty rightly point out that the strength of Pratt's narrative, and of the subjectivity that she creates for herself, rests on her recognition and acceptance of the relationships of power and privilege in which she is embedded. Pratt is able to assume these relationships consciously, in a transformative "rewriting of herself in relation to shifting interpersonal and political contexts" (1986, 210).[3]

What Martin and Mohanty fail to emphasize is the fact that Pratt's narrative is motivated by powerful positive connections that are *not* undermined. Her connections to her lover, to other women, to the feminist movement, to other resistant groups, and even to her parents and her history are what propel her through self-critique and sustain her transformations: her identity. Pratt is very explicit about this. She writes that the process of coming to consciousness about the exclusions and oppressions that underlie each identity has left her close to nonidentity: "As I try to strip away the layers of deceit that I have been taught, it is hard not to be afraid that these are like wrappings of a shroud and that what I will ultimately come to in myself is a disintegrating, rotting *nothing*" (1988, 39). For Pratt, this fear of nonidentity can also be a temptation: if we are members of dominant cultures, "we may simply want to leave our culture behind, disassociate ourselves from it....we may end up wanting not to *be* ourselves" (40).

Against this fear and temptation of nonidentity, Pratt not only consciously assumes the relations of power and privilege that constitute her but also engages in a "positive process" of re-creating herself, of "creating a positive self" (41–2). Pratt does this not just by undermining, but by drawing on and reclaiming her relationships and her past, by strengthening "a sense of connection to history, people, and place" (44), and, importantly, by reaching out to people who are strange to her. Her primary motivation for engaging in this process is love: "How do we *want* to be different from what we have been?" she asks. And answers: "I began when I jumped from my edge…into radical change, for love: simply love: for myself and for other women" (19). Pratt's process began with her love for another woman. For Martin and Mohanty, Pratt's lesbian identity and love for other women serves a unifying function in the text only insofar as it is "that which makes 'home' impossible, which makes her self nonidentical" (1986, 202). But they are wrong. This love, for Pratt, is what motivates her to create a positive identity in connection with others. And what sustains her is the desire, and the need, to "expand her circle of self," to "loosen the constrictions of fear," and to "escape the loneliness of separation" (1988, 19).

While she comes to realize that her dream of a home—an identity—that she could share with all women was based on ignorance and denial of relations of power and privilege among women, Pratt does not give up on her desire to create a new home—a new identity—through connections with others. She does, for a while, withdraw from feminist politics into a sort of seclusion, and a sense of hopelessness. But she reaches out again, to find new ways of connecting with other women, with members of other oppressed groups, to continue a process of self-creation through expanding her circle of self. She does this by actively engaging with people very unlike herself, by learning more about the relations of power that connect her to them, and by learning about their histories of resistance.[4]

Martin and Mohanty's oscillation between identity and nonidentity, home and not home, does mirror a similar oscillation in Pratt's text: while Pratt writes that her engagement in a process of change began "when I jumped from my edge.…into radical change, *for love*" (10) she also writes that she sustains her process of change by trying to stay on the edge, resisting the desire for a safe and comfortable identity: "I will try to be at the edge between my fear and outside" (18). Thus she does oscillate between affirming nonidentity—staying on the edge, risking openness to future, questioning and resisting her identity—and moving from her edge into identification with others, with herself, with a commitment to a specific process of change. There is an ambivalence in the text, as she moves between these two poles. But it seems to me that she does not in fact undermine her identity when she opens herself to question, to recognition of her embeddedness in relations of power. She undermines, rightly, any faith that she had in a simple, too-comfortable identity: she comes to see that this is an identity resting uneasily on top of repression and denial. But because she consciously assumes those power relations, and practically engages with them, she integrates them into her identity. She becomes aware that they have in fact always been a part of her (objective) identity—the truth of herself—and is able to integrate them into her subjective identity—her self-understanding—and thus into a transformed identity that integrates subjective and objective. Thus, her openness becomes not an undermining but an expansion of her self, through a process of positive self-creation: through practical connections and through reflection on them.

Pratt's relational identity, then, is constituted by both relations of power and relations of mutuality, flourishing, and love. She becomes conscious of relations of power only through risking the dangers of love. And she sustains her self through the uncovering of her power relations, and through the risk of non-identity, through forging and remembering and embracing connections. I want to argue, then, for a conception of identity as relational because it is constituted through both relations of power and relations of mutuality and love. They are intertwined, but neither cancels out the other. Neither can be reduced to the other. Nor do they exist only in radical opposition, or oscillation. While Pratt does oscillate between affirming positive connections and uncovering relations of power, she is able to transform her identity only by integrating the two: by engaging with and connecting with others, opening her self to connection with others, she is able to learn about the relations of power that both connect her to and divide her from others, and this knowledge leads to stronger, more aware, and deeper connections. She does not thereby resolve differences or eradicate power. But she does create a stronger, deeper, more connected, more open and knowledgeable identity. And this kind of identity finds a home in the space where the risk of connection is understood to be worth the struggle.

From Private vs. Public to Freedom in Relationship

The third value that Young espouses is the value of *privacy*. Against feminist critics who point out that the private sphere has served only to confine women, to restrict their access to the public realm, Young argues for a distinction between the "private sphere" within which women are confined, and "privacy," which refers to "the autonomy and control a person has to allow or not allow access to her person, information about her, and the things that are meaningfully associated with her person" (162).[5]

But women's confinement to the private sphere and the ideal of privacy as a condition of autonomy are in fact intimately related. Pratt uses the image of the woman entombed in the household in Edgar Allen Poe's "The Fall of the House of Usher" to show that the protection of the white woman in the Southern U.S. Christian household has served (and still serves) to protect the autonomy and control the privacy of whites over the Blacks and Jews who are perceived as threatening. The woman entombed in the household symbolizes the purity that white men are able to protect and keep inside, while projecting all sources of danger, of filth and defilement, onto the others—the Blacks and Jews who are kept outside. "I am entrapped *as* a woman, not just by the sexual fear of the men of my group, but also by their racial and religious terrors," Pratt writes (1988, 38).

As Young notes, Bonnie Honig criticizes the ideal of "home" as "a means of withdrawing from politics into a place of more certain principle and integrity" (Young 1997a, 158).

> The dream of home is dangerous, particularly in postcolonial settings, because it animates and exacerbates the inability of constituted subjects—or nations—to accept their own internal divisions, and it engenders zealotry, the will to bring the dream of unitariness of home into being. It leads the subject to project its internal differences onto external Others and then to rage against them for standing in the way of its dream—both at home and elsewhere. (Honig quoted in Young 1997a, 158–59)

Honig argues, Young writes, that "the sense of home as a place where one is confident who one is and can fall back on a sense of integrity depends on a vast institutional structure that allows such a luxury of withdrawal, safety and reflection for some at the expense of many others who lose out in the global transfer of benefits" (157). Honig argues, then, for engagement in the messy processes of politics in the public realm and against retreat into private spaces of certainty and integrity, autonomy and control. Like Bernice Reagon, Honig argues that feminist politics requires an engagement in risk and conflict with others, rather than retreating to "barred rooms," to a policing of borders that protects us against them.

Young agrees with these critiques of home as a fantasy of wholeness and certainty, and as protection of the private and personal from the political. Nevertheless, she argues that while privacy and the autonomy it affords *can* be predicated on exclusion and terror, they are not necessarily so. In earlier work, Young argued along the lines of Honig and others that autonomy is a "closed concept, which emphasizes primarily exclusion, the right to keep others out and to prevent them from interfering in decisions and actions" (Young

1990, 251). In this earlier work, Young distinguishes between autonomy, which refers to privacy, in the sense that modern corporations are private, and empowerment, which she defines as an agent's participation in social and political decision making. "Empowerment is an open concept, a concept of publicity rather than privacy" (251). At the same time, she defends a conception of autonomy as freedom from interference and control over one's own actions and decisions (250). In "House and Home," Young cites Anita Allen (1988) to argue that while it is true that privacy law has been used to protect the power of male heads of households over women and children, the appeal to privacy as a value for all persons as individuals exposes the extent to which women's privacy is invaded, and provides a source of critique and support of privacy for women (Young 1997a, 163). Certainly, the right to bodily integrity and to decisional privacy with respect to intimate relations are privacy rights that carry special weight for women. Moreover, Young argues, autonomy involves ownership or control over a space of one's own and belongings of one's own, allowing a person to have "control over access to her living space, her meaningful things, and information about herself" (163). Young stresses the importance of material supports for one's identity.

In "House and Home," Young argues that home "enacts a specific mode of subjectivity and historicity" through the "materialization of [one's] identity," in two ways: "(1) my belongings are arranged in space as an extension of my bodily habits and as support for my routines, and (2) many of the things in the home, as well as the space itself, carry sedimented personal meaning as retainers of personal narrative" (149–50). The meanings embedded in the belongings in one's home reflect one back to oneself, and allow one to sustain one's identity. Thus, autonomy or control over one's personal space is essential for creation and maintenance of one's identity. Similarly, in "A Room of One's Own: Old Age, Extended Care, and Privacy" (2005) Young stresses that privacy entails not just decisional privacy, but material personal space of one's own. Noting that residents of homes for the elderly often have no private space for their personal belongings, or for themselves, Young argues that without material personal space of their own, protected from social interventions, the elderly are denied the privacy of bodily integrity and the material support of meaningful belongings that provide the comfort and support for personal habits and the capacities for memory, reflection, expression, and intimacy that are essential to identity. Thus Young argues for a valuation of home and the privacy it affords as "the material anchor for a sense of agency and a shifting and fluid identity. This concept of home does not oppose the personal and the political, but instead describes conditions that make the political possible" (159). It is not immediately clear, however, how Young's conception of autonomy based on privacy escapes this opposition between the personal and the political, the private and the public.

Liberal conceptions of autonomy and privacy are rooted in the Lockean model of the individual and individual freedom, based in the ownership of private property. With the advent of modern capitalism, ownership of private property became the foundation of autonomy understood in terms of rights in competition with others. Against this model of autonomy predicated on private ownership of the household and the self in opposition to and competition with others, Jennifer Nedelsky and other feminist theorists have argued for a model of *relational autonomy*.[6] In some of her essays, Young draws on this body of work to distinguish between personal autonomy and self-sufficiency (1997b, 124–27; 2002, 45–47). In these essays, she defines personal autonomy (which she differentiates from moral autonomy) as "being able to determine one's own projects and goals, how one will live one's life, without having to answer for those goals to others, and without having to obey the orders of others about how one will live" (2002, 45). While in modern liberal capitalist societies the ideal of autonomy is tied to the ideal of self-sufficiency or private ownership of property, Young argues for a conception of autonomy that is instead related to "supportive interdependence" (46). Certain forms of dependence and interdependence, she argues, should be understood "as *normal* conditions of being autonomous" (47). But her conception of autonomy is still liberal, based on negative freedom and hence privacy. Personal autonomy, she writes, "is conceptually close to liberty; where liberty is about simple non-interference" (45). She adds that "personal autonomy carries the additional meanings of being able to decide one's own goals and their means to fulfillment, and meeting with respect from others in one's right to govern one's life" (45).[7] I agree with Young that a capacity for autonomy, which includes privacy from political and social intervention (negative freedom), needs to be affirmed as a condition of political participation, even while we recognize the importance of critiques of withdrawal into privilege and certainty. But we must also go beyond the defense of privacy, to reconsider what kind of autonomy we want and what kind of home would serve as its condition. This means going beyond both critiques and defenses of privacy to a reconsideration of home as a ground for freedom: for relational autonomy.

Drawing on the Hegelian-Marxist tradition, on feminist theories of relational identity, and particularly on the "love and justice tradition of Black America" invoked by Patricia Hill Collins, Cynthia Willett offers a vision of freedom that is situated in relationship and rooted in "home," understood not as ownership of property but as a source of connection with others and a nurturing of spirit. In the love and justice tradition of Black America, Willett finds an "alternative modernism" according to which the focus of freedom and of rights is not the self-interested individual, but the "individual-in-rel ationship-with-others" (2001, 174).[8] Quoting John Edgar Wideman: "Who better to know what freedom means than the slave?" Willett draws on the slave narratives of Frederick Douglass for this alternative vision (Wideman quoted in Willett 2001, 157). For Douglass, "freedom does not reside pri marily in individual or collective forms of ownership or control…Freedom lives or dies in the relations forged between persons" (Willett 190). Douglass offers a reconceptualization of freedom through the metaphor of home (194).[9] Against the modern Euroamerican tradition in which the develop ment of freedom and autonomy is predicated on leaving home, on separation from the mother, Douglass points out that "the practice of separating chil dren from their mothers…is a marked feature of the cruelty and barbarity of the slave system" (Douglass quoted in Willett 2001, 197). For Douglass, freedom was located in the childhood home he shared with his grandmother, a source of a social and ethical force that he calls "spirit" (Douglass quoted in Willett 2001, 190). And his eventual release from slavery was not a sufficient condition for freedom. Freedom could be found again only when he was able to find a new home, in meaningful and supportive relations with others.

To develop this alternative vision of freedom, Willett draws on the work of Patricia Hill Collins, who quotes the words of the ex-slaves Sethe and Paul D, in Toni Morrison's *Beloved*. For Sethe and Paul D, freedom is "a place where you could love anything you chose" (Morrison 1987, 162; Collins 1990, 182; Willett 2001, 179). This understanding of freedom goes *beyond situating freedom in the context of relationships* (the project of most theorists of relational autonomy) to argue that *freedom is precisely the capacity to be in relationships that one desires: to love whom and what you choose to love.*[10] In *Beloved*, Sethe expresses her new-found capacity for freedom to love as an expansion of her self: "I was big…and deep and wide and when I stretched out my arms all my children could get in between. I was *that* wide."(Morrison 1987, 162) Freedom, then, is understood to be not a withdrawal into self-ownership, but an expansion of self in relation-ship. Thus, freedom entails not leaving home, but expanding oneself to find a home "beyond your little meager human-body-mouth-talking all the time" (Reagon 1983, 352). Thus, the most fundamental and crippling form of alien-ation is alienation from love, from erotic power, and from the capacity to hear and to feel one's own desires (Willett 2001, 176–78).

Perhaps this way of understanding freedom—freedom to love, to be in relationships one desires, and to expand oneself through relationship—can help draw out the implications of Iris Young's defense of home as a source of privacy and autonomy. When Young argues that everyone needs a space of her own, belongings of her own, and control over that space and those belongings, she is arguing not only that everyone has a right to noninterference and ownership, but that underlying this right is the need and the right to engage in a relationship with herself that is mediated by her relationship with her belongings—with belongings that reflect her back to herself. The understanding of the self in relation to herself, mediated by objects, takes us back to Hegel and to Marx's 1844 "Alienated Labour." We can add that what is needed is the freedom to love and care for herself, to love those objects that are meaningful to her, that contribute to her life story. And that this love, rooted in relations first experienced in the home, is the source of her love for and connection to other subjects and objects beyond this first home: connections to people, values, work, and social causes, and resistance to oppression. And these connections enable her to create new homes.

From Past vs. Future to Reinterpretive Preservation and Transformative Identification

This brings us to the last value Young identifies: for Young, home is ideally a site of *preservation* of individual and collective history and meaning.[11] Young notes that Simone de Beauvoir (1952) relegates the preservative activity of care for home, for belongings and for children, to women's situation of passivity and immanence, as opposed to the meaning-making work of active, transcendent historical actors.[12] Because Beauvoir associates historicity with futurity, Young argues, she is unable to recognize the work of preservation, of preserving the living meanings of past history, as meaning-making work. Similarly, Hannah Arendt distinguishes between the repetitive, cyclical activity of labor and the meaning-making activity of work. And Martin Heidegger, while recognizing that building requires both constructing and preserving, "drops the thread of preservation and concentrates on the creative moment of constructing" (152). Against these oppositions of meaning-making, future-oriented activity and the passive, past-oriented work of preservation, Young argues that "the particular human meanings enacted in the historicality of human existence depend as much on the projection of a past as of a future" (152). The work of preservation entails the continual renewal of meaning that allows individual and collective identities to be sustained and developed.

Like Beauvoir (and Arendt and Heidegger), Biddy Martin and Chandra Mohanty, Teresa de Lauretis, and Bonnie Honig have all tended to valorize life "on the edge," open to the risk and danger of the future, in opposition to the preservation of home. In Pratt, too, the life of risk and refusal of home is often reminiscent of the will to transcendence of the existential hero. De Lauretis expresses this ideal in her argument that feminists must make a shift in historical consciousness that entails "a displacement and self-displacement: leaving or giving up a place that is safe, that is 'home'... for another place that is unknown and risky" (De Lauretis 1990, 138; Young 1997a, 158). "Life on the edge" is valorized over connection to community and home, over love and desire: "Can I maintain my principles against my need for the love and presence of others like me?" Pratt asks (1988, 50). But we need to question this opposition between principles and the need for love, to ask whether being true to one's principles necessarily requires suppressing needs, rejecting connection, and leaving home. And while Martin and Mohanty may be right to note that by itself the desire for home and community renders feminists indistinguishable from members of the Ku Klux Klan (1986, 209), we need to question the implication that the critique of this desire is what would distinguish us.

Against these too-simple oppositions, Young argues for a distinction between the activity of preservation and the nostalgic fantasy of a lost home.

> Preservation entails remembrance, which is quite different from nostalgia. Where nostalgia can be constructed as a longing flight from the ambiguities and disappointments of everyday life, remembrance faces the open negativity of the future by knitting a steady confidence in who one is from the pains and joys of the past retained in the things among which one dwells. Nostalgic longing is always for an elsewhere. Remembrance is the affirmation of what brought us here. (154)

Young stresses that preservation *can* be conservative, but it can also be reinterpretive: "the narratives of the history of what brought us here are not fixed, and part of the creative and moral task of preservation is to reconstruct the connection of the past to the present in light of new events, relationships, and political understandings" (154). This activity of "reinterpretive preservation" is similar to Pratt's "rewriting of herself." But, as I have argued, Martin and Mohanty (and often Pratt herself) have understood this process as a "conscious assumption" of past identities so that these can be undermined: an oscillation between taking on and undercutting identities and homes. This "conscious assumption," moreover, sometimes resembles a Christ-like martyrdom, as the burdens of the past are taken on, but without redemption. On the other hand, Young's argument that the preservation of the past produces a "steady confidence in who one is" through the "affirmation" of our histories is not entirely adequate either. Pratt can hardly "affirm" the racism, anti-Semitism, sexism, and homophobia that have constituted her identity. Nor can Holocaust survivors and descendants of slaves "affirm" the entirety of their histories. But these histories must be preserved. The question is, how can preservation of such histories lead to something other than utter despair? The preservation of those histories, through the telling and retelling, to ourselves and to others, in ways that will transform us and transform the future, becomes the only way we can hold ourselves together. These retellings affirm both our resistance and our belonging. This understanding of "reinterpretive preservation" makes sense of Young's inclusion, in "House and Home," of the story of her mother, which is also her own story—a story of loss, abandonment, guilt, and forcible displacement. Young writes that she has included this story to preserve the memory of her mother, and to "describe in concrete terms how disciplinary standards of orderly housework and PTA motherhood continue to oppress women, especially single mothers" (1997a, 135). In retelling the story, Young is engaging not in simple "affirmation"—for surely she cannot simply affirm her mother's suffering or her own—but in an act of reinterpretive preservation that not only preserves her mother's memory but also connects her to her mother, and holds herself together, in a way that is redemptive.

I would argue that we can find in this work of reinterpretive preservation a model (certainly not the only model!) for feminist politics and solidarity. Through the telling and retelling of our stories to ourselves and to each other, we combine the conscious assumption of the oppressions and violence that have shaped us with the affirmation of belonging, and the transformation of the future. In doing this, we are not simply affirming our identities or our homes, nor are we rejecting them to leap into the negativity of the future. Nor are we oscillating between affirmation and negativity, or resolving this opposition. We are engaging in a process of transformative identification: through reinterpretive preservation we transform ourselves, and hold ourselves together, through struggle, and without denying any of the suffering and tragedy this entails.

Young's ideal of reinterpretive preservation, then, offers the possibility of connecting past and future. Bernice Reagon expresses this possibility in what she calls "an old age perspective" (1983, 348). And Frederick Douglass expresses it as well, in his vision of freedom as a home for the extended family of humankind—a home in which the spirit will thrive (Willett 2001, 202). As Pratt writes, this dream of freedom, of home, is a childish place, but it is also not a childish place. It is important to hold onto an ideal of a world in which all of us could have such homes.

In the next chapter, I draw on the conceptions of individual and collective transformative identities developed in these first two chapters, to argue for a feminist transformative identity politics. This depends on understanding identities not as categories but as nonappropriative, transformative identifications with ideals, with each other, and with a feminist "we."

Notes

1. Unless otherwise noted, parenthetical citations are to Young 1997a.
2. According to this model, identities are relational because they are defined through relation to what they are not.
3. De Lauretis refers to this rewriting of self as "transformative" (1990, 136).
4. Lugones discusses identification with others as resistant agents (2003, 84–5).
5. In "A Room of One's Own," Young cites Anita Allen's definition of privacy as a condition of restricted access: "Personal privacy is a condition of inaccessibility of the person, his or her mental states, or information about the person to the sense of surveillance of others" (Allen quoted in Young 2005, 164). Young does not clearly distinguish between privacy and autonomy.
6. See Nedelsky 1989, 2011; Mackenzie and Stoljar 2000.
7. Young is alluding here to conceptions of autonomy as positive freedom, in John Stuart Mill's *On Liberty* (1859) and in theories of recognition. Young also recognizes that liberty must be understood as freedom from domination.
8. Willett argues that this alternative understanding of freedom "resonates with a theme of social justice that lies buried in ancient European, African, and Asian texts" (2001, 162). In particular, she argues that it corresponds to an Ancient Greek understanding of social justice, where injustice is seen as the violation of sacred social bonds: hubris (162–63).
9. Willett draws this argument from Andrews 1987.
10. Willett is critical of the concept of autonomy; I am arguing that the conception of freedom she offers can be understood as relational autonomy.
11. Young draws on the work of Sara Ruddick (1989) and Joan Tronto (1992), who focus on preservative love and care for persons. Young argues that this concept should be extended to the preservation of meanings through care for belongings in the home.
12. I criticize Beauvoir's equation of agency with negativity in Weir 1996, 14–25.

3 GLOBAL FEMINISM AND TRANSFORMATIVE IDENTITY POLITICS

Identity is about binding, and it means, on the one hand, that you can be bound—parochialist, narrow, xenophobic. But it also means that you can be held together.

CORNEL WEST

Identity...can be constituted only through acts of identification.

CHANTAL MOUFFE

The coalition requires that we conceive identification anew.

MARÍA LUGONES

Feminist theorists have learned a lot, in the past couple of decades, about the dangers of binding identities. We have learned about parochialism, narrowness, xenophobia; about essentialism and ahistoricism; and about how careless and solipsistic conceptions of who we are can produce exclusion, and suffering, and blindness. We have learned, and continue to learn, crucial lessons about the dangers of collective identities and identity politics. But perhaps we have too often forgotten, or trivialized, or ironized the importance of being held together.

In our work on collective identities, we have tended to reduce the complexity of identity questions to questions of *category*, and thus we have paid too little attention to other important questions: these questions I want to gather under the umbrella of *identification-with*: identification with others, identification with values and ideals, identification with ourselves, as individuals and as collectives. In other words, we have focused too much on the "objectivity" of the category (for example, is the category "woman" essential or constructed?) and too little on the subjectivity of identifications. This leaves us—and I am going to be pointedly vague about exactly who "we" are—without a theory of an affective, ethical, existential ground for solidarity, and therefore, for politics.[1]

In particular, I want to argue that the dimension of identity as identification-with has been the liberatory dimension of identity politics, and that this dimension has been overshadowed and displaced by a focus on identity as category. Moreover, I think that feminist theorists have tended to draw back from the identifications with each other and with shared values that are essential for solidarity, in part because of a false belief that these identifications commit us to a conformity to some preexisting identity category. In fact, I think the reverse is true: our identifications, our commitments and values—our solidarities—shape our designations of identity. For we participate in the constructions of our identities.

In this chapter, I want to reconsider the question of identity politics and its relation to feminist solidarity, in the context of global, transnational feminism. I shall argue that global feminist politics, however multiple and differentiated, require a rethinking of identity politics. This requires a shift from a focus on identity as category to a focus on identification-with. And this involves a shift from a metaphysical to an ethical and political model of identity; from a static to a relational model; from a model of identity as sameness to a model of identity that focuses on what matters, what is meaningful for us—our desires, relationships, commitments, ideals. Finally, it requires a shift to a model that can take account of change: a model of *transformative identity politics*.

This chapter is divided into six parts. In part 1, I argue that feminists have been able to recognize common interests among women only because women's identity has been constituted or constructed by feminists oriented toward solidarity, practicing three kinds of identifications: identifications with ideals, with "we"s and with each other. We do not simply find ourselves belonging to the same category; we are historically engaged agents constructing shared interests, experiences, identities out of very disparate realities. So identity politics cannot be based just on "positional" or category identity. Identity politics are politics of identification. In part 2, I argue that this understanding of identity politics relies on a Hegelian-existentialist model of identity as orientation to meaning: as a question that can be answered only with reference to our attachments and commitments—our identifications. This is a model of identity not as sameness, but as a historical process of holding together: not through stasis, but through transformation. In parts 3 and 4, I take up two feminist texts first published in the late 1980s, both reissued in 2003, to consider their implications for transformational identity politics. In part 3, I address Chandra Mohanty's critique of identification as a ground of solidarity. I argue that while Mohanty is right to criticize an appropriative model of identification based on assumed sameness, she is wrong to reject identification altogether, in favor of coalition. I discuss some false dualisms that emerge in Mohanty's contrast between identity politics and coalition. In part 4, I draw on Maria Lugones's vision of a reconceived identification, and argue that "traveling to the other's world" might be interpreted as a form of transformative identification: an identification based not on presumed sameness, but on recognition of the other, and an openness to transformation of the self. I argue that a transformative identity politics must incorporate both relations of identification and recognition of relations of power: thus, transformative identity politics are politics of self-critique and self-transformation, and transformation of a "we." Finally, in parts 5 and 6, I draw on several theorists to give some content to my understanding of identification with a feminist "we" and with feminist ideals.

Feminist Politics of Identification

In the years before her death in 2004, Susan Okin wrote some very controversial papers on the relationship between feminism and multiculturalism, arguing that universal feminist goals must transcend cultural differences. In a paper on the global movement for women's human rights, Okin argues, with considerable impatience, that during the past couple of decades, while Western feminist theorists have been preoccupied with differences among women, and criticizing any general claims about women as essentialist, feminist activists in the Third World have been making remarkable progress in working together to identify common issues shared by women around the globe, to develop an international movement for the recognition of women's rights as human rights.

> Holding hearings in their own countries, meeting and networking in regional and subregional groups, and then combining their knowledge at international meetings, groups from Africa, the Asia-Pacific region, and Latin America, as well as those from more economically developed parts of the world, were finding that women had a lot in common. They found that discrimination against women; patterns of gender-based violence, including domestic battery; and the sexual and economic exploitation of women and girls were virtually universal phenomena. (Okin 2000, 38)

Certainly, it is ironic that, if we are to accept Okin's analysis, it's the subordinate groups who are affirming women's unity while the more privileged are deconstructing it. But of course, Okin's claim that Western theorists and Third

World activists have been at cross-purposes must be challenged. Okin fails to note that Third World activists have long been frustrated and angered by the tendency of white Western (Northern) women to dominate international feminist politics.[2] It is in response to this anger that Western theorists (and Okin notes that this category includes many "feminists of Third World origins" like Chandra Mohanty) have begun to learn to focus on differences and to challenge universalizing generalizations about women. Thus this theoretical focus on difference has been part of a larger process during which Western participants in international political movements have begun to listen to and learn from those who have been silenced, and to recognize their own roles in the international politics of exploitation and oppression. In her impatience to affirm universal feminist goals, Okin misses the history and diversity of feminist theorizing. Okin wants to affirm a simple, universal women's identity as the basis of universal interests and goals. But the history of questioning and critique, and the shift of the subject of feminism from center to margin, has produced a far richer, more complex, and truer understanding of who women are and what their interests might be.

Still, I take Okin's point to be that Western feminist theorists have been so preoccupied with deconstructing the category of women that we have largely failed to notice that global feminism is happening, or to support that movement with a theoretical reconstruction of feminist identity politics. Okin is only partly right. Reconstructive work is certainly being done. Ironically, Mohanty, whom Okin singles out as one of the academics failing to contribute to global feminist politics, has focused her work on reconstructing a "feminism without borders," through analyzing local struggles and moving from the local to the common interests that link Third World women, and all women. Mohanty argues for a transnational feminist politics focusing on decolonization and anticapitalist critique, along with critiques of "the interwoven processes of sexism, racism, misogyny, and heterosexism" (C. Mohanty 2003, 3). Many other theorists are developing analyses of the intersections of multiple sources of oppression, and their implications for feminist practice.[3] But while much of this work affirms feminist solidarity, most theorists avoid attempting to reconstruct identity politics for feminism.[4]

Other contributions to the volume of essays in which Okin's essay appears (Narayan and Harding 2000) do touch on this question. In particular, Ann Ferguson's model of bridge identities and negative identity politics and Alison Jaggar's work on the global feminist discourse community are important contributions to this discussion. And important interventions have been made by Paula Moya, Linda Alcoff, Satya Mohanty, and others formulating postpositivist realist theories of identity to reclaim identity politics.[5] The most influential theoretical model of women's identity politics that could support an international movement for women's rights is the "positional identity politics" cited by Ann Ferguson (2000, 200) following Alcoff (1988), Teresa De Lauretis (1987), Denise Riley (1988) and bell hooks (1990). Ferguson describes positional identity as

> an identity we find ourselves assigned to by social definition, usually by opposition to another social category, such as "women" = "not-man" .... We can develop an identity politics based on this social positionality that resists constituting a new essence of femininity.... Instead, we can constitute our politics by agreeing with others defined by a similar positionality to fight for certain social justice demands, such as abortion rights, freedom from male violence, affordable childcare, or adequate research on women's health issues. (Ferguson 2000, 200–201).

Gayatri Spivak's "strategic essentialism" is based on this model (Grosz 1984/1985), as is Riley's suggestion, at the end of her book deconstructing the category of "women," that to do politics we must "act as if women existed" (Riley 1988, 112).

"Positionality" can be interpreted in a very thin way, to refer to women's position as a category in opposition to men. This kind of positional identity politics reduces women's identity to a simple matter of category, defined through opposition to another category. While this model avoids positing a shared essence or universal experience, it nevertheless takes women's identity as something that is given and objective. Women's identity is understood to be constituted by various systems, structures, or histories, but for us, it is simply given: we find ourselves assigned to it. And the assumption is that solidarity emerges from recognition of this shared identity.

But a model of women's identity as category is not a sufficient basis for politics. This understanding of identity cannot possibly account for global feminist solidarity around shared issues—or indeed, for any kind of solidarity at all. Women do not feel solidarity with other women because we belong to the same category. To address Okin's point—and Mohanty's—that women around the world seem to have a lot in common, we need to acknowledge shared interests around shared issues, like discrimination, violence, child care, home care, and reproduction. And these shared interests are not simply given and discovered, but are to a large extent constructed through our attention to what is significant and meaningful to us as feminists and through our orientation to solidarity. In other words, *feminist solidarity plays—and must play—an important role in constituting women's identity.*[6]

This understanding of identity is suggested by Linda Alcoff's conception of positionality. Alcoff argues that the concept of positionality includes two aspects: it refers, first, to women's position within a historical and constantly shifting context, to a situation within a "network of relations" including relations with others, with economic conditions, and with cultural and political institutions and ideologies. Secondly, drawing on Teresa de Lauretis's argument that "the identity of a woman is the product of her own interpretation and reconstruction of her history, as mediated through the cultural discursive context to which she has access,"[7] Alcoff argues that the concept of positionality includes women's use of their positional perspective as a location, a place from which values are interpreted and constructed. Thus, "When women become feminists the crucial thing that has occurred is not that they have learned any new facts about the world but that they have come to view those facts from a different position, from their own position as subjects. When colonized subjects begin to be critical of the formerly imitative attitude they had toward colonists, what is happening is that they begin to *identify with* the colonized rather than the colonizers" (Alcoff 2006, 148; my italics). I want to argue, further, that women come to recognize a position shared with other women *very different from themselves* only through an orientation to solidarity that is facilitated by this identification.

For example, to what extent do the American career woman needing access to child care and the immigrant nanny who is denied access to her own children and the mother struggling to feed and shelter her family on the streets of Manila have anything in common? If the issue of child care is something we share, it is shared in very different ways. And not only in different ways: we are related through global care chains in which some of us must take responsibility for the exploitation and oppression of others.[8] In order to find that access to child care, fair wages and working conditions for care workers, the right of immigrant care workers to care for their own children, parenting rights for gay and lesbian partners, and access to housing and social and economic support for caregivers are all related issues; and in order to find that these are related in turn to access to contraception and abortion, and resistance to forced sterilization, and in turn to various forms violence and abuse, and to various forms of patriarchy and heterosexism and capitalism and racism and imperialism, we have all had to learn, and must continue to learn, about the very different life issues faced by women in very different situations. And we are able to do that only because we approach these issues and each other with an orientation to solidarity, through which we construct and interpret our shared interests, through an interpretive framework that is feminist. This process involves at least three kinds of identifications:

1. We identify with—we are passionately committed to—certain values and ideals of social justice that we identify as feminist ideals. This identification develops with the critique of oppression, of unjust power relations, and mediates our understanding of the issues we share in common. Certainly, we do not all identify with the same values and ideals; and certainly, our values and ideals change through history and practice. What is important is that these identifications inform our practices.
2. Our attribution of significance is mediated also by our identification with ourselves—with women, and with feminists—as a "we." In combination with the first form of identification, this translates into an identification with a *resistant* "we." In other words, an orientation to solidarity. (Of course, this identification interacts with identifications with other, multiple "we"s.)
3. This identification with a "we" is connected to particular identifications with each other, involving various kinds of relationships, from erotic desire to love, empathy and admiration for intimates and for strangers. The nature of these relations varies, and they may be variously mediated (some, for example, are mediated by texts or images) but the point is that various kinds of particular identifications, including identifications with others very different from and distant to ourselves, mediate our feminist solidarity, and our collective and individual identities. (And these identifications coexist with conflicts and hostilities.)

Thus to identify issues in common—and to recognize ourselves as belonging to the same category—we have had to approach these issues with a feminist consciousness that combines:

1. an appeal to and identification with feminist ideals
2. an orientation to solidarity—identification with women and with feminists—as a "we"
3. identifications with each other, including other strangers.

I don't mean to suggest that there is no given or categorical identity of women. But this "objective" categorical identity, however essential or constructed, interacts with a "subjective," interest-driven, identification-based relational identity, such that what we have in common is in part a product of our interested interpretations and affective commitments.

I am arguing that an understanding of these forms of identification and their contribution to political struggles opens up a different understanding of identity politics. This different understanding is predicated on a noncategorical conception of identity: not identity as sameness, but an ethical-relational and political model of identity, defined through relationships with other people and through identification with what is meaningful to us, with what we find significant. To understand this we need to shift from our preoccupation with the metaphysical question of the category of women to a different approach to the question, "Who are we?"

Holding Together

Identity is about binding, and it means, on the one hand, that you can be bound—parochialist, narrow, xenophobic. But it also means that you can be held together.

CORNEL WEST

For this alternative model of identity, we can draw, in part, on the Hegelian-existentialist philosophical tradition. We can begin by looking at individual identity. In contrast to the analytic model of personal identity, in which identity is defined as being the same person over time, in the Hegelian-existentialist tradition, the problem of individual identity is a problem of meaning—of the meaning of my life, of what matters to me. As I have noted in chapter 1, this understanding of identity is articulated by Charles Taylor:

> The question "Who am I?" can't necessarily be answered by giving name and genealogy. What does answer this question for us is an understanding of what is of crucial importance to us. To know who I am is a species of knowing where I stand. My identity is defined by the commitments and identifications which provide the frame or horizon within which I can try to determine from case to case what is good or valuable, or what ought to be done, or what I endorse or oppose. In other words, it is the horizon within which I am capable of taking a stand. (1989, 27)

This horizon, formed by the particular attachments, commitments, and identifications that give one's life its significance, is essentially dialogical: we form our identities through our relationships, commitments to and identifications with particular others and collective "we"s.

Here we are entering into an understanding of identity that is not about sameness or category or identity as something. We are not exactly focusing on uniqueness either—although that is a kind of identity very different from identity as sameness, and it gets closer to what we mean. Instead, we are focusing on an understanding of identity with which we are all, in this culture, quite familiar: when I ask, "Who am I?" in the existential mode, I am not asking about the categories I belong to or the characteristics I can enumerate. (These can form part of the answers, but they are not essential to the question.) I am not asking what makes me the same as others, or what makes me unique. I am asking, rather, what matters to me. What is the meaning and significance of my life? In other words, to what and to whom am I attached? With what and with whom do I identify?

When we're talking about identity as meaning, we mean more than denotation. When we talk about wanting a meaningful life, we don't mean that we want to understand facts and definitions. If life has lost its meaning, if we experience anomie or alienation or angst, it is not because we can't remember our name and phone number and what we do for a living. (Or even our gender, color, or sexual orientation.) We're talking about an experience of belonging, of connectedness, of being *held together*. By the values, ideals, commitments, attachments, and relationships that matter to us.

What does it mean to hold oneself together? To hold a self, a community, a social movement together? When we talk about identity in this way, we're talking about a very practical capacity and a desired goal: to keep oneself from falling apart, from being overwhelmed by anxiety or despair, from being crushed by oppression and destitution, disoriented and pulled apart by dislocations; to sustain a community in the face of conflict, oppression, and diaspora; to sustain a social movement in the face of resistance from without and strife and disillusion and fatigue from within. But holding an identity together is, ideally, nothing like maintaining sameness over time. Or enforcing sameness across group members. Holding together requires the opposite: I cannot hold my self together without continual re-creation; the self has to be reconstructed and reenacted every day, through acts of self-making, and self-identification. Communities and social movements can be sustained only through continual rebuilding of relationships, rethinking of meanings and goals, and practices of identification with each other, with a we, with some kind of meaning or significance (which can change over time). Thus although there is certainly a conservative moment in holding together, it's nothing like stasis, and it's not repetition, either.

So we are talking about a historical process of creating meaning over time, through practices of identification. One of these practices is the practice of narrative. Seyla Benhabib argues that a narrative model of identity opens up an understanding of identity of self that does not mean resolving into unity or sameness: "The narrative model of identity is developed precisely to counteract this difficulty by proposing that identity does not mean 'sameness in time' but rather the capacity to generate meaning over time so as to hold past, present, and future together" (1999, 353). The narrative capacity to generate meaning over time is more than a capacity to make sense of one's life. It's a capacity to *identify with* one's life as a life that matters—a life worth living, as Taylor says. It's a capacity to experience one's life as one's own—as, in part, one's own discovery and creation. And it is a capacity to experience oneself as holding together, through connection—to oneself, to one's meanings, to other people, to significant "we"s.

Thus this alternative understanding of identity is *ethical-political*: focused on meanings, values, and struggles for change. It is *historical*: focused on processes of creating meaning through practice and through narratives over time. And finally, this understanding of identity is *relational*: formed through relationships with, identifications with meanings, values, and other people.

It is perhaps not so difficult to accept this understanding of identity when we are considering the identity of a self. But shifting from I to "we" is more problematic for us. We—we Westerners—are a culture of individualists, and we find it difficult to think in terms of "we"s. Many theorists have retreated altogether from thinking about collective identities to a focus on individual identities—as if it's impossible to talk about a collective identity, a "we." We are a culture afraid of the constraints imposed by any "we." We resist; we ironize; we fictionalize and nominalize. But surely, these ironized and nominalized and strategic identities are just as simplistic as unreflective essentializing. And is it really the case that individual identities are any less complex and conflictual than collective identities?

When we talk about a collective identity, are we saying that a "we" must consist of everyone sharing the same meanings, the same history? No: if we do this, we've returned to an understanding of identity as sameness. The focus here is on collective constructions of identity, through identifications, which will inevitably include multiple, and often conflicting, struggles. The focus here is on the orientation to meaning; but it is not necessary—or possible—that we all mean the same things. What is necessary is that we value, and invest in, holding together. Because this valuation, this investment, gives our lives meaning. If we hold to this different conception of identity, then *identity politics* is about *an active historical, political process of identification with, shaping and creating a "we."*

In the Hegelian tradition, identity is understood to be: (1) constituted historically and relationally; and (2) internally complex, differentiated, and conflictual. Thus, collectivities are not given categories but are effects of history, combining historically produced systems or structures with the interested participation of human agents: social struggles. This means that identities cannot be simply given and objective, nor can they be solely products of conscious or intentional choice. As individuals and as collectives we are engaged in a constant dialectic between the identities we find ourselves in and the identities we are creating. More than this, we find ourselves already in *identifications with* meanings, others, "we"s—identifications that are often unconscious, and in spite of intention, but whether chosen or not are intensely meaningful for us. And we develop and transform our identities through these kinds of identifications. Identity politics has always been a complex process involving finding ourselves identified as belonging to a particular category (women, blacks, gays), and identifying with these particular "we"s, and constructing our identity through active processes of resistance, of making meaning, through political struggle, through identifications with each other, through creating new narratives, and thereby (re)creating ourselves, and our identities.

Surely, this relational identity—identity understood in terms of commitments and identifications—is the basis for any viable collective identity, at any level, and hence for identity politics: no collectivity, no "we" actually develops through an assertion of sameness, or category. We develop our collective identities rather through our associations, our relations to each other, and to meanings, worlds, ideals that might be shared. Through identifications that hold us together.

Critiques of Identification: Mohanty and Reagon

Identity... can be constituted only through acts of identification.

CHANTAL MOUFFE

The shift from a focus on category identity to a focus on identification is not, of course, unproblematic. The ideal of identification—with others, with a collective "we," with shared meanings, ideals, and values—as a source of political solidarity, has been strongly criticized by feminists. The models of women-identification proposed in the 1970s by the Radicalesbians and by Adrienne Rich in 1980 met very quickly with critiques, not only for assuming an essentialist identity of women but also for espousing an idealized sisterhood based on simple identifications with each other, and for implying that anyone insufficiently "women-identified" was not a good feminist. And there have been many critiques of the expectation that feminism should involve identification with a set of shared norms and goals.[9]

Here I want to focus on, and respond to, the critique of identification in Mohanty's "Feminist Encounters: Locating the Politics of Experience" (1987). Mohanty's essay was an important intervention in the late 1980s, and remains influential, and relevant, today. It is included, in somewhat revised form, in *Feminism without Borders* (2003). In this essay, Mohanty criticizes Robin Morgan's introduction to her anthology *Sisterhood Is Global* (1984), arguing that Morgan's ideal of global sisterhood is based on an assumption of women's shared interests and experiences across cultures. This model of sisterhood erases power relations, divisions of class and culture, and histories of struggle with a conception of experience as essentially individual, generalized to a preconstituted collectivity of women, immediately accessible and fundamentally psychological. Thus, women can immediately recognize and identify with other women's experience, for experience is a matter of shared feelings, attitudes, and intentions. Mohanty is particularly critical of Morgan's claim that women around the world can "recognize one another." For Mohanty, this assumption "encapsulates Morgan's individualized and essentially equalizing notion of universal sisterhood" (2003, 115). Mohanty argues that "the insistence that we must easily 'recognize one another' indicate[s that] we must identify with *all* women. But it is difficult to imagine such a generalized identification predicated on the commonality of women's interests and goals across very real divisive class and ethnic lines" (115–16). For Mohanty, this ideal of universal sisterhood is a "middle-class, psychologized notion" that relies on "the logic of appropriation and incorporation" (116).

Mohanty does, in this essay, support an ideal of women's unity. She argues, however, that any unity of women cannot be simply given, but must be a political unity that is achieved through the active struggle of women as agents: "I believe that the unity of women is best understood not as a given, on the basis of a natural/psychological commonality; it is something that has to be worked for, struggled toward—in history" (116). And surely Mohanty is right. We cannot assume common experience, feelings, interests, or goals; we must build unity through our practices. Any unity that we achieve will be a unity forged through struggle and conflict—and will need to develop through continuing struggle and conflict. But I am arguing that there must be an orientation to solidarity, emerging out of identifications with each other, with a "we," and with feminist ideals, to motivate and to sustain any struggle for unity.

Mohanty is right to reject the possibility of a simple identification with other women, across nations, cultures, and classes. For Morgan, as Mohanty points out, women's capacity to recognize each other emerges naturally from their universally shared attributes and experience. Thus women's identification with each other is an effect of their membership in the same *identity category*: we all share the same characteristics and experiences, and this is the basis of our identification with each other. Mohanty calls this the "feminist osmosis" theory: feminist politics emerge naturally out of the women's shared experience of oppression. As Mohanty points out, this model denies women's agency, as well as the necessity of theorizing experience, and overlooks the intersecting relations of power in which women are embedded.

Mohanty is right also to criticize an *appropriative* form of identification: when we claim to recognize and identify with others, based on a presumption of shared experience and identity, we render them the *same* as us; we erase their difference, and our relative positions in power relations, and comfort ourselves with an illusion of shared feeling. In fact, then, we are sharing nothing. And the assumption of shared feelings, of a natural, given sameness, removes any need for self-critique or learning about the other.

It's true that this is what too often has been meant by identification with others, in practice. And Mohanty is right that we need to resist this kind of appropriative, leveling identification, based on assumed sameness. But I want to distinguish this kind of identification from a model of identification that is not appropriative and not based on sameness. This requires shifting away from a model of immediate identification to a model of identification mediated by recognition of power relations, and by a desire to engage with, learn about, and be transformed by the other. To clear the way for this alternative model of identification, we need to move beyond some false dualisms that can be found in Mohanty's critique of Morgan, and in the contrast she draws between Morgan's conception of universal sisterhood and Bernice Johnson Reagon's model of coalition.

In her talk addressed to the West Coast Women's Music Festival in 1981, Reagon pointed out that black women could not be so easily assimilated to the preconceived (white women's) category of "women." Mohanty notes that Reagon rejected a model of politics based on a presumed sameness of experience and posited instead a model of experience shaped by politics and by political engagement. Thus Reagon restored agency to feminist politics, and understood this politics as engagement in struggle rather than transcendence of a man-made history. Reagon began from a recognition of racism, rather than a simple affirmation of differences, and argued for a politics of coalition, grounded not on shared oppression but on survival: "You don't go into coalition because you *like* it. The only reason you would consider trying to team up with somebody who could possibly kill you, is because that's the only way you can figure you can stay alive" (Reagon 1983, 357; quoted by C. Mohanty 2003, 117).

Reagon's and Mohanty's critiques of simplistic identity politics are important and have contributed greatly toward the development of much more complex analyses of feminist struggles. But in the sharp contrast drawn between Morgan's universal sisterhood and Reagon's understanding of coalition, between a simplistic identity politics and a coalition of possibly hostile strangers, what emerges is a stark dualism that obscures the possibility of solidarity grounded in any kind of identification.[10] There are at least three problematic dichotomies at work here.

First, Mohanty, with Reagon, contrasts identification characterized by abstract psychologizing, an attribution of shared feelings, with a model of coalition politics characterized by action and struggle. Here, the important truth—that experience is always shaped by politics, and that resistance to oppression requires active engagement in particular struggles—slides into a disparagement of affect: we are to shift the legitimate field of politics from the realm of the psyche, of feeling and emotion, to the realm of action. The idea that we can, perhaps, sometimes recognize and identify with each others' experience and struggles—and that recognition and identification can be important dimensions of solidarity and struggle—is dismissed as middle-class psychologizing. Thus, identification—and recognition—are too simply equated with psychologism and individualism, and with appropriation and incorporation, with an assumption of a preexisting sameness. An alternative model of identification must, then, combine agency, engagement, and political struggle with affective and cognitive relations.

Second, Morgan's claim that we can "recognize each other" is described as romantic, idealistic, lyrical, in contrast to Reagon's hardheaded, even Hobbesian, acceptance of power, of the reality of domination and oppression: coalition entails joining forces with others who might kill us in the interest of self-preservation. To go beyond this duality we need to recognize that our relations might be complex: that we might be located in power struggles, in relations of domination, and still be capable of recognizing and identifying with each other, by, in Maria Lugones's words, "traveling to each others' worlds." So we need a model of identification in coalition that can take account of our locations in power relations. The best feminist theory, along with other critical theories, has recognized the coexistence and interaction of power and oppression with sociality and connection. In the Hegelian-Marxist tradition, contrary to the Hobbesian assertion of the primacy of domination, oppression is regarded as a failure of relationship, a form of alienation—a breakdown, severing connection and identity. But if that sounds still too oriented toward some kind of fundamental unity, then at least we can say that primary relations of power and oppression coexist and interact with mutuality and connection.

Finally, Mohanty, with Reagon, argues that identity politics too often emerge out of a desire for home, for nurturance, and for comfort in sameness. Identities become "barred rooms," places where we can huddle together, safe and protected. These barred rooms must be traded for the acceptance of risk and danger, of engagement in a process of conflict and struggle. This involves "a recognition of the limits of a narrow identity politics. For once you open the door and let others in, 'the room don't feel like the room no more. And it ain't home no more'".[11] Reagon and Mohanty are absolutely right to criticize the desires for control, for appropriation and sameness, and for the policing of boundaries that produce "barred rooms." At the same time, a disturbing trend is emerging here: identity politics are based on desires for home and nurturance, on feelings, on the romantic, idealistic, and lyrical; coalition is based on action, struggle, hardheaded acceptance of power relations and engagement in the risk and danger of politics. We need to be wary of this too-simple repudiation of qualities that are soft and feminized, and affirmation of the tough, masculine world of power. Surely, desires for nurturance, and feelings and ideals, must inform our politics; surely, we should not be too quick to dismiss the dream of a world where all could find homes. As I argued in chapter 2, we need to reconceive identity and home to include difference, conflict, and dissent. Thus, identity politics can become not retreats to barred rooms but affirmations of more inclusive homes.

Transformative Identifications

The coalition requires that we conceive identification anew.

MARÍA LUGONES

In her essay, "Playfulness, 'World'-Traveling and Loving Perception" (1987, 2003), María Lugones describes a kind of identification very different from the kind that is criticized by Mohanty. Where Mohanty understands identification to be an act of appropriation based on a presumption of sameness, and argues instead for a coalition based on recognition of power relations and conflict, Lugones calls for a "deep coalition" based on identifications.

For Lugones, the capacity to identify with another is the capacity to "travel to her world." As I understand it, this model of identification includes a cognitive-epistemic component: to identify with another is to recognize her experience and her meanings, and, importantly, to recognize her resistant agency; and it includes also an affective component: to identify with another is to love her; to "welcome her world," to value her. For Lugones, identification requires overcoming the indifference that maintains lonely independence, and becoming able to see oneself in another. The capacity to see oneself in the other (rather than simply recognizing the other's separateness, independence, difference) is essential for a recognition of our interdependence. Without this, we are "not quite whole."

Lugones is writing, in this essay, to other women of color, arguing that if women of color are to form an effective coalition, it needs to be "deep coalition" (2003, 98), founded on recognition of and identification with each others' *resistant agencies*. Too often, Lugones writes, the resistant agency of the other is obscured by a defensive perception of the other as oppressed, as she is constructed by domination. When the other is seen only as oppressed, identification is blocked: "To the extent that we face each other as oppressed, we do not want to identify with each other, we repel each other" (85). At the same time, "we lack insight into each other's resistant understanding" (84–5). Identification with the other requires recognizing "interrelating 'worlds' of resistant meaning" (85).

While her essay is addressed to women of color, Lugones describes her experience as a woman of color among white/Angla women: too often, "they ignore us, ostracize us, render us invisible, stereotype us, leave us completely alone, interpret us as crazy. All of this *while we are in their midst*" (83). Here Lugones is describing a "failure of identification," an inability or refusal to "see oneself in other women who are quite different from oneself" (82). The other is left to be different, separate, independent; no connection is acknowledged; thus the refusal of identification is a form of *indifference*: "The more independent I am, the more independent I am left to be. Their 'world' and their integrity do not require me at all. There is no sense of self-loss in them for my own lack of solidity. But they rob me of my solidity through indifference" (83). For Lugones, this failure of identification is a failure of love.

Thus while Mohanty and Reagon are right to note that an appropriative form of identification, predicated on a presumption of sameness, indicates a failure to recognize the lines of power that divide us, Lugones suggests that a recognition of difference and of power divides is not enough: if we want to do politics together, we need to cross through the lines that divide us, to take the risk of actively identifying with others very different from ourselves. This means identifying with others who might threaten us; frighten us; others whom we might rather not see and not know. (And perhaps, many of us are all too capable of recognition and critique of power, but not so good at reaching out, to travel to the other's world and actively identify with her.)

Clearly, Lugones is not advocating the kind of identification that Mohanty rejects: this is an identification that is not based on sameness, on identity as belonging to the same category: "To the extent that identification requires sameness, this coalition is impossible. So, the coalition requires that we conceive identification anew" (85).

But what does it mean to conceive identification anew? How can this be identification at all, if it's not based on sameness? I think that what Lugones means by identification becomes clearer once we shift to the alternative model of identity I discussed in part 2 of this chapter: an ethical, relational model of identity as a historical, dialogical process of making meaning. Once we make this shift, we can see an alternative to the dualism of same versus other that underlies critiques of identification: rather than identifying with the other's sameness, or simply recognizing her otherness, we can move to what I am calling *transformative identification*. Transformative identification involves a recognition of the other that transforms our relation to each other, that shifts our relation from indifference to a recognition of interdependence. Thus identification with the other becomes not an act of recognizing that we are the same, or feeling the same as the other, or sharing the same experiences. Identification becomes a process of remaking meaning.

Traveling to the other's world, seeing oneself in another, requires an active process of getting to know the other, through an imaginative and empathic engagement that goes beyond recognizing how we are the same, and beyond "putting oneself in the other's place," without change to the self. This engagement with the other requires learning about her world, learning to take her perspective, and thus forever changing my own.

I want to argue that this kind of identification transforms our identities: through identification with the other we transform ourselves, and we construct a new "we": a new identity. When I identify with you, I am reconstituting myself, my identity, through traveling to your world: through coming to know you, by listening to, witnessing your experience, I am expanding my self to include my relation to you. But rather than assimilating you into myself, assuming sameness, or simply incorporating your difference without change to myself, I am opening my self to learning about and recognizing you: I cannot do this without changing who I am. And because this process changes our relationship to each other, it also changes you—more so, of course, if the process of identification goes both ways. Through this relationship, we are changing who we are: we are creating a new "we"—a new identity that includes all of our differences and all of our relationships. We are learning to hold ourselves together.

Because this is a relational model of identification, it relies on a different conception of the self, and of a collective "we," from the individualist model Mohanty rejects. This kind of identification involves an opening up to difference—an expansion of the self, through an enlargement of one's horizons. This conception of identity is not atomistic but interconnected, because identity is understood only through relations to ideals, others, and multiple "we"s.

Because a transformative identity politics involves identifications across power divides, it needs to be grounded in a complex, relational model of identity that can incorporate recognition of *relations of power*, as well as *relations of identification*. A transformative identity politics needs to avoid being simply positive by including reflection and self-critique. Thus, it must involve recognition of my own implication in relations of power. My identity is locatable only in webs of interconnection with others, on a global scale. This understanding of identity draws on the model of universality proposed by Satya Mohanty:

> How do we negotiate between my history and yours? How would it be possible for us to recover our commonality, not the ambiguous imperial-humanist myth of our shared human attributes, ... but, more significantly, the imbrication of our various pasts and presents, the ineluctable relationships of shared and contested meanings, values, and material resources? It is necessary to assert our dense particularities, our lived and imagined differences; but could we afford to leave untheorized the question of how our differences are intertwined and, indeed, hierarchically organized? (1989, 13)

In other words, we can understand a global unity or identity not through some kind of immediate, given shared humanity or shared feeling, but through understanding our relationships in webs of power.

This recognition, I argue, requires a process of transformative self-critique and self-identification: once I recognize that I am in a relation of power with you, I need to re-identify—re-cognize—myself to accommodate that recognition. This process might require another understanding of identification, found in Julia Kristeva's work. In *Strangers to Ourselves*, Kristeva writes that the capacity to identify with other strangers develops through a capacity to identify with our own strangeness: to recognize, and empathize with (affectively accept, feel love for, care for, and commit to) the parts of ourselves that are repressed, abjected, repudiated, or simply strange to us. And perhaps we need to do this if we are in positions of privilege or power: we need to identify with ourselves in that position of privilege, that which we would rather deny, in order to take responsibility for it. (Perhaps we need to do this also to recognize our "shared oppression"—another part of ourselves that we might want to deny.) Ideally, of course, this will also provoke an active process of transforming that power relation, and of transforming our identities.

This re-identification of ourselves through recognition of our positions in relations of power needs to be combined with the kinds of positive identifications affirmed by Lugones. Thus we can understand ourselves to be united in webs of interconnection by both *relations of power* and *relations of identification*. By combining these two models, I think we can combine our need to risk engagement with difference, and to recognize our positions in relations of power, with our need to be held together—both as individuals and as collectives. And we can combine a recognition of the conflicts and struggles that connect us, and a utopian vision for a future, and a home, that all of us can share.

What then might a transformative feminist identity politics look like? I have argued that a transformative identity politics involves a practice of transformative identifications with each other, through which we constitute ourselves as a "we." And this practice interacts with our identifications with the "we," and our identifications with feminist ideals. In parts 3 and 4 of this paper, I have focused mainly on identifications with others across lines of power, to produce new, more complex and differentiated "we"s. To conclude, I would like to elaborate a bit on the other two kinds of identification, which, I believe, are necessary for transformative feminist identity politics.

Identification with Feminists as a Resistant "We": Orientation to Solidarity

In several early interventions into feminist debates, feminists of color argued that any genuine solidarity among feminists must be founded on plurality, on recognition of relations of power, and on dissent and disagreement, rather than on assumed agreements that in fact exclude (Moraga and Anzaldua 1981, hooks 1984, Mohanty 1987, Anzaldua 1990, Mohanty, Russo, and Torres 1991, Lugones 2003). In *Solidarity of Strangers*, Jodi Dean draws on some of this work to present a conception of a communicative "we" that is not based simply on an opposition to a "them," nor simply on membership in an identity category.[12] Dean argues that in the wake of critiques of and struggles over identity politics, we need to reconceptualize solidarity: this requires moving beyond both "conventional solidarity," which presupposes a single shared history and tradition or set of interests and values, and "affectional solidarity," which is based on intimate relationships and feelings. Dean's alternative, more suited to modern democratic and global cultures, is "reflective solidarity": a form of solidarity founded on ties created by dissent.[13] Drawing on Lynet Uttal's account of her experiences in Anglo and Women of Color feminist groups, Dean argues that questioning and critique provide a stronger basis for solidarity than assumed agreement. Uttal found that in the Anglo feminist group, it was assumed that solidarity required agreement. But this assumption actually worked to silence dissent and conflict. In contrast, in the "feminists of color" group, "questioning and disagreement enabled each woman to take part in the construction of the group's 'we'" (Dean 1996, 31).[14]

Thus, Dean argues that rather than severing connections and destroying the "we," dissent and critique are the foundations of a communicative "we." This "we" is constructed through communicative practice: "through language we establish a relationship, creating a common, social space." Thus the communicative "we" is very different from a "we" founded on membership in a category that is opposed to another category. This "we" is internally constructed, through dialogical practice, through relationships to other members of the "we." The communicative we "stresses the possibility of an inclusive understanding of 'we' whereby the strength of the bond connecting us stems from our mutual recognition of each other instead of from our exclusion of someone else." This "we" is not founded on opposition to a "them."

There remains, nevertheless, a resistant aspect to this "we." According to reflective solidarity, "We call on another to stand by us over and against an 'other' who seeks to oppress us or who fails to recognize and include us. So here, reflective solidarity refers to the exclusion of exclusion: we are connected through our struggle against those who threaten, denigrate, and silence us" (31).

While Dean stresses that the communicative "we" is constructed through dialogue, I want to stress that this "we" is possible only through an orientation to solidarity, a commitment to and identification with a "we." As Dean explains, "Reflective solidarity refers to *a mutual expectation of a responsible orientation to relationship*" (29). The focus here is on some form of commitment to holding together—not through suppression of critique, nor enforcement of stasis, but through engagement, commitment to working through, together.

Dean intends her model of reflective solidarity to be an alternative to identity politics. I, however, want to draw on this model to distinguish between an identity politics based on category identity and assumed sameness, and a transformative identity politics based on transformative identifications. When identity politics rest on an assumed sameness and agreement, the effect is a silencing that is, in fact, a form of dis-identification: I keep my disagreements, my questions, my discomfort to myself, and thus I dis-identify with the "we," disengage and draw back into myself. The identity of the "we," then, is a false identity, based on an agreement and a sameness that do not in fact exist. A transformational identity politics rests on the engagement and identification of each participant with the "we": if I identify with this "we," it matters to me to engage in questioning and critique, to continually rethink, and thereby reaffirm, the basis of our attachment. (Similarly, if I identify with feminist ideals, it matters that I get them right—and to do this, I need to open my understanding of these ideals to questioning and critique.) Moreover, identification with a "we" (like identification with each other and with ideals) means that we value the "we" (the other and the ideals) enough to expose ourselves to uncomfortable truths and to engage in self-critique and transformation.

Many theorists argue that a process of disidentification is necessary in order to transform identities, and I am agreement with this (Alarcón 1990, Butler 1993, Muñoz 1999, Medina 2003). Identities must be questioned and criticized and queered if they are to be transformed. The subject of feminism as defined by middle-class straight white western/northern women has been and continues to be challenged by feminists of color, two-thirds-world women, lesbian, queer, and transgendered people, and by men, among others. As I argued in chapter 1, these challenges typically depend on identifications with alternative identities, such as those listed above, and sometimes it is important to shift from the challenged identity to the alternative one, to reject the challenged identity and move on. But if the challenged identity is worth fighting for, then disidentification must provoke transformation of that identity. This is why the identity of the feminist subject has been challenged and contested: so that it can be transformed. This kind of disidentification is different from the dis-identification to which I refer above in that it involves a challenge and confrontation, rather than silent withdrawal. I am arguing that this confrontation involves taking the risk of connection, and of re-identification, motivated by a critical identification with the identity or collective in question—by a desire to be part of a transformed "we." Only an identification with that "we"—only the conviction that the identity in question is worth fighting for, and worth transforming—can open up the "we" to the possibility of a genuine solidarity based on diversity, rather than presumed unity.

Given this understanding of identity politics, I wonder if perhaps the fear of identity politics has emerged not just out of a fear of restrictive categories—a fear of closure and exclusion—but also out of a fear of the necessity, in any collectivity, of opening up—to deeper relations to others, to self-critique, to inclusion of difference, to the risk of participation, conflict, and dissent. For all of these often difficult and dangerous forms of opening up are essential to identification.

Shared Feminist Ideals?

I do think that global feminism, in the present, can and should be oriented toward identifications with some broadly shared values and ideals. As Cheryl Johnson-Odim wrote in her contribution to *Third World Women and the Politics of Feminism*, "The fundamental issue for Third World women is not generally whether there is a need for feminism..., but rather what the definition and agenda of that feminism will be.... The need for feminist theory and organization is clear" (1991, 319).

> But there is a broad base on which First and Third World feminists must agree if feminism is truly to be concerned about redressing the oppression of women. This broad base must at least recognize that racism and economic exploitation are primary forces in the oppression of most women in the world. It must acknowledge that while gender is a potential bond, women participate in the oppression of other women all over the world. It must respect different cultures, and it must agree that women in various places are perfectly capable of having their own voice. This can be a beginning. It must also strive to see the world through noncolonial eyes.... We must stop reproducing pictures of the world only from the inside out, and try to look from the outside in. (325–26)

Mohanty has echoed and extended this position in *Feminism without Borders*, arguing that transnational feminist politics must focus on "decolonization, anticapitalist critique, and solidarity."

So in this political/economic context, what would an economically and socially just feminist politics look like? It would require a clear understanding that being a woman has political consequences in the world we live in; that there can be unjust and unfair effects on women depending on our economic and social marginality and/or privilege. It would require recognizing that sexism, racism, misogyny, and heterosexism underlie and fuel social and political institutions of rule and thus often lead to hatred of women and (supposedly justified) violence against women. The interwoven processes of sexism, racism, misogyny, and heterosexism are an integral part of our social fabric, wherever in the world we happen to be. We need to be aware that these ideologies, in conjunction with the regressive politics of ethnic nationalism and capitalist consumerism, are differentially constitutive of all our lives in the early twenty-first century. Besides recognizing all this and for- mulating a clear analysis and critique of the behaviors, attitudes, insti- tutions, and relational politics that these interwoven systems entail, a just and inclusive feminist politics for the present needs to also have a vision for transformation and strategies for realizing this vision.

Hence decolonization, anticapitalist critique, and solidarity (Mohanty 2003, 3).

This vision is compatible, I think, with the agenda of the struggle for inter- national women's rights as human rights documented and promoted by Okin (2000). This does not, of course, mean that these and other visions of feminist ideals can be combined without dissent and conflict, or without transformation.

Looking back at the history of feminist theory and practice, it seems to me that we—feminist theorists and activists—have been engaged in the pro- cess of reconstituting ourselves, as women and as feminists: creating a trans- formed women's identity politics. The arguments put forward by Mohanty and Lugones, and by generations of feminist theorists, have been taken up in both feminist theory and feminist practice: they have helped all of us to transform who we are, how we do politics, who we understand ourselves to be. They have helped us change our understanding of our goals, our visions of the future, our relationships with each other. Transformative identity politics are, I think, already happening.

In the next chapter, I discuss the ways in which transformative identity politics have produced and transformed, and continue to transform, the iden- tity "women."

Notes

1. Naomi Scheman makes this point: "Resistance is connected to solidarity, which is a matter of identifying *with,* rather than *as*" (Scheman 1997, 147). See also Scheman 2011.

2. I retain the term *Third World* here because both Okin and Mohanty use it. See Mohanty's discussions of the use of this term, in *Feminism without Borders* (2003).

3. See, for example, Grewal and Kaplan (1994), Shohat (2001), Narayan (1997), and Moghadam (1994). All of this work develops out of a political orientation different from, and more complex than, Okin's. For Okin, global feminist politics (by which she means the struggle for the recognition of women's rights as human rights) requires rejecting the claims of "culture." For Mohanty and the theorists cited above, global or transnational feminist politics must focus on multiple and interlocking oppressions.

4. But there are important exceptions. See Hekman 2005, Heyes 2011.

5. See S. P. Mohanty (1993, 1997), Moya and Hames-Garcia (2000), Moya (2002), Alcoff (2006), Alcoff, Hames-Garcia, Mohanty, and Moya (2006). See also Marilyn Frye 1996.

6. Naomi Scheman similarly argues that the solidarity produced through *identification with* shapes identity, citing the example of the reshaping of lesbian identities through solidarity with gay men in the era of AIDS: "My sense is that AIDS-related politics has greatly increased the numbers of lesbians who identify with gay men, and that lesbian identity has, as a consequence, been reshaped. Whom one identifies with is inseparable from what one identifies as." (Scheman 1997, 147). See also Scheman 2011.

7. de Lauretis 1986, 8–9; cited by Alcoff 2006, 148.

8. See Hochschild (2000, 2002) and Weir (2005) on global care chains.

9. See Phelan (1989) for an excellent discussion of these early critiques. See also Heyes 2011.

10. This dualistic opposition between identity and nonidentity, home and not home, runs through "Feminist Politics: What's Home Got to Do With It?" (Mohanty and Martin 1986). I discuss this opposition in chapter 2.

11. C. Mohanty 2003, 118; quoting Reagon 1983, 359. Note that in the original essay Mohanty wrote "the limits of identity politics." This is qualified as "a narrow identity politics" in *Feminism without Borders.*

12. Dean draws from Jürgen Habermas (1979) to develop her model.

13. While Dean argues for a shift from conventional and affectional forms of solidarity to reflective solidarity, I want to stress that both conventional and affectional dimensions can be incorporated into reflective solidarity. As I have argued, identification with a "we" of women and/or feminists requires that we hold on to affectional solidarity—solidarity involving feelings or affect—as an important dimension of a transformative identity politics.

14. See also Iris Young's arguments for the importance of differences as resources rather than obstacles for communicative democracy: "I propose that we understand differences of culture, social perspective, or particularist commitment as resources to draw on for reaching understanding in democratic discussion rather than as divisions that must be overcome." (Young 1997c, 60) Young further argues for an expanded conception of democratic communication that includes greeting, rhetoric, and storytelling. See also Young 2000.

4 TRANSFORMING WOMEN

Only the exaggerations are true.

THEODOR ADORNO

Maybe not.

CAT POWER

I just want to be a woman.

PORTISHEAD

No one wants to hear, again, the question "What is a woman?" Surely the question has been discussed to death, and should be laid to rest and never reopened again.

But then, Simone de Beauvoir said the same thing in 1949. "For a long time I have hesitated to write a book on woman. The subject is irritating, especially to women; and it is not new. Enough ink has been spilled in quarrelling over feminism, and perhaps we should say no more about it" (Beauvoir 1952, xix). Beauvoir did, of course, go on to say quite a bit about it. She begins the second paragraph of the Introduction to *The Second Sex* with the question, "But first we must ask: what is a woman?" So I feel that I am in good company. But the question I want to ask is somewhat different. My question is this: How is it that feminists have come to accept that the identity "women" is solely an effect of subjugation? [1]

To answer this question we need to go back, again, to Beauvoir. For it was Beauvoir who famously argued, in *The Second Sex,* not only that "one is not born, but rather becomes a woman"—not only that the category "women" is socially constructed—but that "woman" is constituted through subjugation. Woman is the Other, is not-man, is lack, is object, subordination. The argument that "woman" has been constituted as man's Other has been foundational for feminism. But while Beauvoir argued that it was entirely possible for women to challenge and to change the social norms that produce "woman" as subordinated Other, it is not surprising that her argument that woman *is* the Other has been taken as the foundation for feminist arguments that the essence of the identity of women is subordination. This argument is made very clearly by many radical feminists: as Amy Allen points out, Catharine MacKinnon, Andrea Dworkin, and Carol Pateman all "explain differences between men and women as a function of domination: in their view, relations of domination are prior to differences between men and women, and the emphasis on difference is introduced after the fact for the purpose of justifying and maintaining that system of dominance. Differences between men and women, then, are simply the reified effects of dominance" (Allen 1999, 11). Thus, MacKinnon argues that "the organized expropriation of the sexuality of some for the use of others defines the sex, woman" (MacKinnon 1982, 2)[2] In her groundbreaking "The Traffic in Women," the structuralist anthropologist Gayle Rubin argues that the system of gender is a system of oppression, and that "we are not only oppressed *as* women, we are oppressed by having to *be* women" (Rubin 1975). In "One is Not Born a Woman," Monique Wittig argues that "woman" is not a natural category but is rather "the *mark* imposed by the oppressor." (Wittig 1992, 11). With the French feminists the equation of "woman" with subjugation, and the understanding of this subjugation as constituted through the binary logic of identity, is introduced into poststructuralist feminisms, and is repeated in the work of Judith Butler. Butler draws on Beauvoir, Rubin, Wittig, Irigaray, Derrida, Lacan, and Foucault to argue that gender is an effect of systems of patriarchy, phallogocentrism, and compulsory heterosexuality, all of which she understands to be emanations of the singular logic of the metaphysics of substance, which is the binary logic of identity. Thus, Butler argues not that woman is simply an effect of subjugation but that gender, the subject, and identity are effects of subjectification, which is equated with subjection. But since the category of women is produced only through these multiple, but ultimately singular, regimes of power, to be a woman is to be subjected to these regimes. Hence, once again, woman = subjection, and subjection = subjugation.[3]

I don't want to detract from the truth of any of these theories. Patriarchy and phallogocentrism and compulsory heterosexuality do constitute "women" as subjected and subjugated. I want to argue that while the argument that the identity "women" is an effect of subjugation was intended to defend against substantive definitions of women, *the equation of women with subjugation, constituted through the binary logic of identity, has become itself a substantive definition*. My "Women and Gender Studies" students, by the time they graduate, have learned to take for granted that woman *is* subordination. Which puts them, and all of us who identify as women, into a position that is deeply paradoxical, and I think, unliveable. I want to stress here that I am speaking from my own experience: I am questioning theoretical formulations that have been central to my own understandings of women and gender, and hence central to my own self-understanding.

Once woman is defined as an effect of subjugation, any call for the emancipation of women ensnares us in what has been called the paradox of freedom: as Judith Butler puts it, "the category of 'women,' the subject of feminism, is produced and restrained by the very structures of power through which emancipation is sought" (Butler 1990, 2). This argument is echoed by Wendy Brown, who writes that "it is freedom's relationship to identity" that "yields the paradox in which the first imaginings of freedom are always constrained by and potentially even require the very structure of oppression that freedom emerges to oppose" (Brown 1995, 7). For some, this leads to the argument that the emancipation of women requires that we must be, in Nancy Fraser's words, "weaned from our attachments" to our identities as women (Fraser 1997, 31). Here Fraser echoes the radical feminist Ti-Grace Atkinson, who wrote: "those individuals who are today defined as women must eradicate their own definition," in effect "commit suicide," in order to give birth to themselves as "individuals."[4] This solution is psychically problematic, to say the least. I find it a bit daunting that Monique Wittig, to support *her* argument that women must commit suicide as women, cites Virginia Woolf, who wrote that to be a writer a woman must first kill "the angel in the house." Killing the angel in the house is one thing, but if we are to use the words of Virginia Woolf to support the argument that women must commit suicide to emancipate ourselves, we should perhaps remember that Virginia Woolf really did kill her*self*. And perhaps this is not a coincidence.

So I want a different solution. For me, a better solution to the paradox of women's identity is to change our understanding of what women's identity is. Several theorists, including Linda Alcoff (2006), Sally Haslanger (2000), and Marilyn Frye (1996), have argued that to do this we need to develop a better, postfoundationalist, realist metaphysics of identity.[5] I want, instead, to move out of metaphysics, into a more pragmatic understanding of women's identity as constituted through multiple and conflicting and contesting relations.

Judith Butler does start to head in this direction. She argues that for the radical and French feminists, the understanding of the identity "women" as only the effect of subjugation is dependent on a totalizing model of *the social* as a coherent and homogeneous system of domination. In *Gender Trouble,* Butler criticizes this model, and argues instead for an understanding of the social as structured through multiple sites and relations of power. Unfortunately, Butler, following the early and middle Foucault, in combination with Derrida and Lacan, sees the social as constituted through *only* disciplinary regimes of power that emanate from an originary law: we are constituted, as subjects, through interlocking regimes of subjectification, all of which are subsumed under a single logic, which is the logic of identity. Resistance is understood in terms of the theory of performativity, according to which identities are resignified through citations that subvert and redirect. This seems to open up the possibility of fluid and contesting relations of power. Thus, in places Butler argues for the possibility that "'women' designates an undesignatable field of differences, one that cannot be totalized or summarized by a descriptive identity category" and argues that "then the very term becomes a site of permanent openness and resignifiability" (Butler 1992, 16). Here Butler opens up the possibility of "women" as a site of productive contestation: "I would argue that the rifts among women over the content of the term ought to be safeguarded and prized, indeed that this constant rifting ought to be affirmed as the ungrounded ground of feminist theory. To deconstruct the subject of feminism is not, then to censure its usage, but, on the contrary, to release the term into a future of multiple significations" (Butler 1992, 16).[6] Thus, "*woman* itself is a term in process, a becoming, a constructing that cannot rightfully be said to originate or to end. As an ongoing discursive practice, it is open to intervention and resignification" (Butler 1990, 33). I support entirely this understanding of *woman* as a term in process, open to intervention and resignification. Yet for Butler these interventions and resignifications must always cite and repeat the normative law of identity: must "call into question the regulatory practice of identity itself" (Butler 1990, 32). Thus every iteration and every performance of the identity "women" requires a repetition of the originary law, the "violence of the letter, the violence of the mark" that produces "women" as subjected (Butler 1992, 17). This is the paradox: that the possibilities opened up are always in opposition to the formative law of identity itself. Phenomenologically, this means that the subject must risk absolute incoherence, unintelligibility, in order to signify differently. But I think that this is a misrepresentation of what identities are, and how they are constituted. The assumption is that the identity "woman" is an effect of a law of identity that constitutes "woman" through opposition to "man"—or vice versa. I want to argue that the identity "woman" is multiply constituted through multiple relations, and that the binary opposition man/woman is just one of those relations.

This binary, structuralist account of what identity is does not solve the paradox of identity, but remains within it. I want to affirm Butler's call for an opening of the term "women" to multiple possibilities. To do this, however, we need to question the assumption that identity originates in the law, and that the identity "women" is always an effect of that law. To get out of the paradox of identity we need to change the terms—to broaden and complicate our understanding of what identity is. We need to move, then, to an understanding of the social as a site of multiple and contested practices and relations—of power, but not only of power. Of subjection, but not only of subjection. Thus, identities are sites of multiple and contested and conflicting (and not just interlocking) relations of various kinds, and these include not only relations of subjectification but also relations of recognition and identification, of flourishing, of meaning, of love, of different kinds of power, including empowerment and solidarity. Identities are historically produced through these multiple and conflicting relations, and these multiple and conflicting constitutive relations of identity are *not reducible* to disciplinary regimes of subjection.

Here I want to argue in particular that the *identity of women* is constituted through multiple and conflicting relations, and thus our agency is enabled not only through relations of power that cite the law but also through other kinds of relations—and not only through the dominant norms that enable as they constrain, but also through norms that contest: norms of alternative and resistant and marginalized cultures and communities. I am arguing that we need to move out of our preoccupation with the identity of women as a fixed category, constituted by a fixed binary logic of identity, and out of our understanding of the question of the identity of women as a metaphysical question, into an understanding of the identity of women as an effect of our practices, and of multiple and conflicting relations. The identity "women," then, is not a fixed concept: not only is its meaning produced differently in different contexts (as Cressida Heyes, drawing on Wittgenstein, has importantly argued) but it is an effect of all of our connections and relations—to each other, to the world, and to multiple "we"s. Only such a complex conception of identity can make sense of our experiences of the *conflicts* inherent in being women. And only such a complex conception of identity can render our desires and motivations to be women as something other than just false consciousness, or attachment to false idols—and thus can support an agency that does not require self-negation. This is important, because a woman's capacity to *criticize* oppressive conceptions of "woman" depends to a large extent on her capacity to access alternative interpretations. Those alternative interpretations frame alternative women's identities—subversive and *resistant* identities. As I argued in chapter 1, her capacity to access these alternative interpretations will depend to a large extent on her *identifications with* those alternative, resistant identities, with alternative defining communities. I am particularly interested in women's collective practices of saying "we" as practices that constitute and transform the identity of women. Further, I understand women's identity in terms of an interrelation between the "objective" and the subjective, between who we are and who we understand ourselves to be; between how we are constituted and how we participate in constituting ourselves. Thus, I shall argue that to move beyond the paradox of identity, and the paradox of freedom, we need to transform women: to transform ourselves and the concept "women."

In this chapter, I argue for an understanding of "women" not only as an effect of subjugation, and not only as an effect of a binary law of identity, but as an effect of multiple contesting and conflicting relations. In the following two sections, I first argue that there are good reasons for a transformative reconstruction of the identity "women," and then criticize the construction of the identity "women" in opposition to freedom, and argue for a rethinking of "women" in relation to an alternative conception of freedom in relationship. In the second half of the chapter, I take up Linda Zerilli's Arendtian argument for a political re-creation of women through women's practices of freedom, and argue for an understanding of these practices as transformations of the identity "women."

But Why Should We Transform Women?

But wouldn't it, after all, be better for women, and all of us, to thoroughly ·deconstruct and dismantle gender, to move into the future by creating something new, rather than settling for reworking the old identity of women? The recognition of multiple genders and the "invention" of queer and transgender as alternative gender possibilities has surely been a good thing, not only because these provide a place for those of us who do not fit easily, or at all, into the categories male or female, but also because, once we have recognized that *none* of us fits so easily into these categories, that in fact the effort to live up to the categories can be psychically excruciating, the possibility of "deconstructing" or queering the categories and opening up to a proliferation of gender possibilities is liberating.

The tremendous importance of queer and transgender theories in opening up the possibilities of gender is unquestionable. The work of biologists like Anne Fausto-Sterling, and of transgender and queer theorists who deconstruct the gender binary and argue for the existence of multiple sexes, genders, and sexualities, and for a proliferation of genderings, open up possibilities for individual and collective practices of freedom that were once unthinkable.[7] But while the queering and proliferation of gender categories offer new ways into the future, the transformation of women is another, equally creative, and important way—especially given the vast numbers who continue to identify as women, and who are oppressed as women. And I do not think that these ways are mutually exclusive. I think that we can take up diverse and multiple directions, as complementary strategies of emancipation. If we shift our understanding of the identity "women" from fixed category produced through a binary logic to fluid identity produced through multiple relations and practices, an identity whose meanings are complex and contradictory, an identity that changes with our changing practices, then escaping the identity "women" is no longer necessary for liberation. And that is because citing an originary law that defines the identity "women" is no longer necessary for our agency and freedom as women. The struggle to conform to rigid gender norms can be seen as only one aspect of gender performance. If those rigid norms are no longer definitive of gender identity, but are only one aspect in a spectrum of meanings, then gender performances that are compelled by conformity to norms are not the only ways in which gender is deployed, and change can come from other sources besides resignifications of an originary law, or failures to cite norms properly.

So there are several good reasons for engaging in a project of transforming "women" rather than leaving that identity behind. As I have already suggested, the first reason is that women need to find a way forward that does not involve self-negation. As Butler notes, we are constituted *as* gendered subjects; there is, at this point in our history, no simple gender-neutral subjectivity. So the gendering goes very deep—is essential to the self. This may be changing; but so long as we are deeply constituted as gendered, the negation of our gender without an alternative that is both viable and desired is self-negation.

For Butler, the constitution of gendered selves is a melancholy story. Gender is the constraint that enables, the violence without which we could not be, the subjection that allows subjectification: that allows us to be selves at all. Thus, we have to accept the grim reality that we can't just escape our genders, that we can only rework the identities through citations that fail to repeat properly, and thereby hope to subvert the identities through exposure of their artifice. I agree with Butler that gender goes that deep, and I agree that it can be psychically excruciating. I do not agree that this is all that gender is, and I do not agree that becoming gendered selves is necessarily and only a process of subjection to disciplinary regimes, according to the binary logic of identity. So this is my second reason—that our construction as women is not one-dimensional, is not just the imposition of a law or category, but is complex and multidimensional, and historical. And thus we can transform women without simply repeating an oppressive norm. This leads to my third reason: that women are, and always have been, active participants in our construction as women. We are participants not just in the sense that we repeat norms, but in the real sense that we are active, reflective, agents, as individuals and as collectivities. We are participants in our history, and feminist solidarity is an important part of that history. We are, and have always been, engaged in the ongoing project of constituting "women."

Fourthly, I want to make the perhaps radical suggestion that much of what we have created, as women, has been good. And that's why the desire to be women is not just false consciousness. When I presented earlier versions of this chapter as a paper I was surprised by the number of women—feminists— who confessed that they could not imagine defining women as anything other than the effect of subjugation, or subjection. Nor could they imagine defining woman outside of the binary of man/woman. But what have we been doing in our women's studies programs, associations of feminist philosophers and academics, feminist movements, lesbian communities, women's cooperatives, and culture-building and other alternative communities if we haven't been transforming women: producing women as something other than subjected? And aren't we being constituted, as women, through feminist and women's art and literature and film, and through desiring and identifying with alternative ideals and figures of women—sweatshop union organizers, guerrilla girls, African grandmothers, mannish lesbian mothers are creating conflicting, alternative meanings for "women." It may be argued that the existence of all kinds of women is no argument against the fact that the concept or category "women" is produced through the binary logic according to which woman is constituted as not-man, and as subjected. But I am arguing that that logic is inadequate to account for the complex and conflictual nature of our gendered constitution. These different meanings and norms are constituted through different and conflicting logics of identity and identification, and not just through resistances enabled by subjection. Thus, the identity women is not just a grim reality that we must accept and/or subvert but also a good that we have created, and continue to create. That's why there's conflict.

It should also be pointed out that the identity "women" is being transformed not only by women, but by other relations and discourses, including interactions with men, and by queer and transgender and transsexual communities, cultures and discourses. And this is happening not only in the margins. Once transgendered people are the subjects of Hollywood movies and "pregnant men" are appearing on Oprah surely no one can see women, or gender, in quite the same way again. Of course there are massive defenses and resistances, but the seeds of doubt have been planted, and our understandings of gender—and hence of what women are and can be—are getting shaken up. This means that "woman" can no longer be understood so easily as "not man."

Finally, I think that transforming women can and should coexist with creating queer alternatives, because we have a lot of unfinished work to do in the name of women. And that this work requires solidarity among women—saying "we" as women. I will say more about this later.

What's New? Identity as Entrapment and as Freedom

For all of these reasons, I think that we need to question the understanding of the identity of women as a trap, and this requires a rethinking of our understanding of identity in relation to freedom. Biddy Martin has expressed concern about a tendency "to construct 'queerness' as a vanguard position that announces its newness and advance over against an apparently superseded and now anachronistic feminism with its emphasis on gender." While she affirms the importance of queer studies, she writes, "But I am worried about the occasions when antifoundationalist celebrations of queerness rely on their own projections of fixity, constraint, or subjection onto a fixed ground, often onto feminism or the female body, in relation to which queer sexualities become figural, performative, playful, and fun. In the process, the female body appears to become its own trap, and the operations of misogyny disappear from view" (Martin 1994, 104). Martin argues, then, that the argument that queer must supersede women as the subject of the future is predicated on a conception of women, and of the female body, as a trap, as subjection, and that this view obscures the relations of oppression that cannot be subsumed under the production of gender itself—obscures, then, misogyny, or patriarchy, and the oppression of *women*.

Jay Prosser repeats Martin's critique of the valorization of a new playful queerness over old, static gender categories, and connects this to a critique of the association of identity with domestication. Prosser argues that queer theory's deconstruction of gender categories relies on a deployment of transgender that elides homosexual desire with transgender identification. "In its earliest formulations…queer studies can be seen to have been crucially dependent on the figure of transgender" (Prosser 1998, 21). Queer studies relies on the trope of crossing, illustrated by the transgendered subject who is seen to be crossing several boundaries at once: "both the boundaries between gender, sex, and sexuality and the boundary that structures each as a binary category" (21–2). Thus, Prosser argues, transgender is idealized as a queer transgressive force, identified with queer transgender identity. Crucial to this idealization is "the consistent decoding of 'trans' as incessant destabilizing movement between sexual and gender identities. In short, in retrospect, transgender *gender* appears as the most crucial sign of queer *sexuality's* aptly skewed point of entry into the academy" (23).

Prosser traces this connection through central texts of queer theory, and back through earlier gay and lesbian studies texts. In particular, Prosser argues that Judith Butler's *Gender Trouble* relies on and enables a syllogism: transgender = gender performativity = queer = subversive. "If *Gender Trouble* enables the syllogism transgender = gender performativity = queer = subversive, it stabilizes this syllogism through suggesting as constant its antithesis: nontransgender = gender constativity = straight = naturalizing. The binary opposition between these syllogisms proliferates a number of mutually sustaining binary oppositions between *Gender Trouble's* conceptual categories: queer versus straight; subversive versus naturalizing; performativity versus constativity; gender versus sex" (33).

Prosser argues that the elision of queer with transgender and the equation of transgender with the subversion of gender amounts to an appropriation of transgendered and transsexual subjects for queer purposes. "What Butler does not consider is to what extent—and on what occasions—transgendered and transsexual subjects and methodologies might not wish for inclusion under the queer banner" (58). As Prosser points out, "there are transsexuals who seek very pointedly to be nonperformative, to be constative, quite simply, to *be*" (32). Butler's essay "Against Proper Objects," Prosser writes, "assesses inclusion and the resistance to inclusion solely from the perspective of queer; it does not imagine possible resistance stemming from the putatively excluded 'sexual minorities.'... In the case of transsexuality there are substantive features that its trajectory often seeks out that queer has made its purpose to renounce: that is, not only reconciliation between sexed materiality and gendered identification but also assimilation, belonging in the body and in the world—precisely the kinds of 'home' that Butler's essay holds at bay in its critical troping of 'domestication.'" (58–9). Gendered identities, for Butler, are traps that imprison us in domesticity, in straight boring homes. "Since *Gender Trouble*, 'domestication' has figured as something of a spectre in Butler's work. Domestication appears to represent the assigning of subjects and methodologies to specific categorical homes, the notion that there is an institutional place to which they belong" (59).

While I think it is true that Butler does tend to deploy queer as both the source and the telos of the deconstruction of binary gender categories, I don't think we can fault Butler for holding out the possibility of the kind of happy playful queerness to which Biddy Martin refers: Butler's story is, it seems to me, relentlessly melancholic. While compulsory heterosexuality produces melancholic subjects (and surely Butler is right about this) queerness does not offer redemption, for queerness is no escape from subjection. The possibility of a happy playful queerness is, however, the conclusion drawn by many of Butler's readers, and is implied in much of queer theory.

And Prosser is right to note that for Butler the desire for belonging and home only leads to *entrapment* in static, domesticated identity categories that have been imposed upon us by repressive regimes. In contrast, Prosser notes that the narrative used by many transsexuals to describe their experience is the narrative of escape from the wrong body, the wrong identity, into the right one. In other words, identity is a trap only if it's the wrong identity. These narratives can be, and often are, dismissed as naïve and conformist repetitions of desire for old and oppressive gender categories, as failures to escape the trap of identity for something else. But this interpretation discounts the fact that what is being expressed in these narratives is an understanding of *freedom* very different from freedom as escape from the trap of home. The desire for belonging and home in the right body, the right gender identity, is a desire for freedom from the wrong body, freedom in a body, an identity, where one can be finally at home.

Similarly, narratives of coming out (as gay, lesbian, queer, or transgendered) are typically narratives of escaping the darkness and isolation of the closet into the freedom of an identity in a community where one feels finally at home. Butler dismisses such narratives when she writes that coming out is merely the transition from one identity-closet to another (Butler 1991). But this dismissal fails to differentiate between an identity in which one feels alienated and unintelligible and an identity in which one feels more at home. And this is an important distinction. Surely one of the goals of queer theory and activism, despite the focus on subversion of home, is to create a space, a home, where queerness can belong: to create homes that are spaces of freedom for queer identities, and for new gender or genderless possibilities that have yet to be imagined.

In *Queer Phenomenology,* Sara Ahmed writes that "orientations are as much about feeling at home as they are about finding our way." Leaving home allows us to learn what home means: "homes are the effects of the histories of arrival" (Ahmed 2006, 9). For Ahmed, "loving one's home is not about being fixed into a place, but rather it is about becoming part of a space where one has expanded one's body, saturating the space with bodily matter: home as *overflowing* and *flowing over*" (11). This alternative image of home as an expansion of oneself and one's body into space is, I want to argue, an alternative image of *freedom*.

Writing of her own experience of changing her sexual orientation in midlife, Ahmed notes that for her, becoming queer has meant becoming disoriented, but it has also been a process of reorientation. "Becoming a lesbian still remains a difficult line to follow," she writes, because "the lesbian body does not extend the shape of this world, as a world organized around the form of the heterosexual couple" (20). Still, becoming a lesbian is a process of reorientation. "Becoming reorientated, which involves the disorientation of encountering the world differently, made me wonder about orientation and how much 'feeling at home,' or knowing which way we are facing, is about the making of worlds" (20). Ahmed compares this "making of worlds" to her experience of migration across countries and cultures: "migration involves reinhabiting the skin" (9). This process of reorienting through reinhabiting the skin is a central theme for Prosser, who quotes the female-to-male transsexual Raymond Thompson, writing of hir experience of inhabiting the "wrong" female body: "Since my body is not my own I cannot feel the warmth of it, so I am cold, very cold on the inside.... I could simply never be comfortable and warm in my own skin.... There is a sense of *disconnectedness* and unreality, of being left out in the cold."[8] It should be stressed here that the understanding of identity as domestication completely ignores the tremendous risks involved in transitioning to a new identity, of whatever kind.

Perhaps, then, the desire for an identity in which one feels at home is not best understood as a desire to conform to a category that entraps, but is better comprehended as a desire for a *connection*. For a better, more meaningful and enabling connection that allows one to expand oneself in relation to a space, a body, a world where one can feel at home. This might be a desire for a connection with one's body that one can affirm. And the implication is that the desire for that connection is a desire for *freedom*—for a freedom not in escape from home or identity, but the freedom that can only be experienced when one finds oneself at home in the world: when one feels a connection with one's body, and with oneself, that one can affirm. I don't think this experience is simply reducible to conformity to oppressive gender norms. And it is not necessary to argue that one's relation to one's body can ever be free of conflict and suffering to draw a distinction between better and worse relations, relations that I can and cannot affirm.

Similarly, the experience of coming out as gay or lesbian, or queer, or transgendered, is not best understood as simply another conformity to an oppressive identity category—is not, then, simply the move from one closet into another one, but is a move from isolation toward connection. This experience is perhaps better understood as the process of discovering and making connections with others in a community in which one's identity—at least one of one's identities—is affirmed, and reconnecting with oneself in a new world where one can be intelligible. Thus, gay and lesbian identities are not just oppressive categories, not just new closets, but are sources of connection, attachment with each other and with a community, that are in turn sources of freedom. It is not necessary to romanticize community as a utopia free of pain and conflict to recognize its importance as a source of freedom. So while of course there will be conflict and trouble in any community, and there will never be a community where every part of one's self will be intelligible and accepted, a community where one's gender and/or sexuality is affirmed is a lot closer to freedom than another closet. Moreover, a community in which one of my most significant identities is affirmed provides a ground for the renegotiation of this and other identities in this and other communities.

As Prosser's argument suggests, queer theorists too are motivated not only by a desire to subvert and escape identities but by desire for and identification with a new queer identity: an ideal of queer/transgender that could displace old identities. Thus queer theory itself suggests the possibility of another kind of identity, an identity that would not be a rigid category, but would be a source of freedom in new connections/reconnections with our bodies, ourselves, and each other.

Once we shift to an understanding of identities as not just epistemological categories but significant connections, then the question of identity is not just a question of how I have been constituted by norms and laws but is the question: to whom and to what am I importantly connected? One's connections to one's body, to locations of place and history, to desired others, to others with whom one identifies, to communities in which one can feel more at home, to what we care about—all of these connections are the substance, the embodiment of our identities. And these questions are not reducible to each other. Our connections and interdependencies are not reducible to regimes of subjection. Once we shift to this understanding of identity then we can understand the desire for belonging and home in identities not as a conformist acceptance of imposed and static identity categories but as a desire for connection realizable through the creative constitution of fluid and complex yet shared identities in relation with others. We can understand, moreover, that the (re)creation of these identities involves not just conformity and capitulation but the *risk* of connection. If we shift to this conception of identity then we can understand *freedom* not just as escape from imposed identities but as finding and forging connections that we can affirm.

To return to the question of women's identity: the paradox of women's freedom arises because identity and freedom are conceived as opposites: because the identity "women" is conceived as a trap, as subjugation, and hence as opposed to freedom. If we shift to a conception of identity as constituted not through a singular and totalizing logic of subjection but as constituted through multiple and conflicting logics, practices, and relations, including the practices of feminist communities, and if we shift further to an understanding of identity as not just imposed category but meaningful connections, then identity is no longer opposed to freedom, and freedom is no longer paradoxical. Freedom can be found in the discovery and creation of connections—identities—that we can affirm.

I would argue that freedom is the condition of being in relations that one can critically affirm. If identities are effects of our connections and relations, then freedom from rigid identity categories requires freedom through *identifications*. As I have argued in chapter 1, our capacity to *criticize* oppressive conceptions of ourselves depends to a large extent on our capacity to access alternative interpretations; and those alternative interpretations frame alternative identities—subversive and *resistant* identities. And these can include alternative and subversive and resistant women's identities. And our capacity to access these alternative interpretations will depend to a large extent on our *identifications with* those alternative, resistant identities, with alternative defining communities. Thus, freedom is always through but also *to* or *towards* a community or a place where I belong, for we are ourselves only through our connections, and our connections are our identities. So, while re-creating ourselves and our world may require that we criticize all of our defining communities, this does not mean that we necessarily escape them, but that we renegotiate our connections. And we need to do this in order to get past the false individualism of modern culture, to discover and develop our freedom as fully social beings.

It seems to me that this is the liberatory potential—a potential that has been all but erased from our memory—in the early radical lesbian feminist figure of the women-identified woman. This figure has been extensively criticized as essentialist and exclusionary; while these critiques have been important, they have occluded the radical potential of theories of women-identification. What these theories offer is a critique of the definition of women solely in terms of relation to man—as not-man, other, negative—and the suggestion that we can redefine and re-create women through relations among women. They offer a critique of the definition of woman as an effect of subjugation, and open the possibility of a transformation of who and what women are, and who we understand ourselves to be. They offer, then, a critique of the binary logic of identity, and open the possibility of reconstituting identity through our practices. Thus, they offer the possibility of a shift from a meta-physical to a political definition of women.

Adrienne Rich argued that women might be able to create new connections with other women, and with ourselves, by revaluing the connections between and among women that have existed through history. Thus, identifying with other women, and with ourselves as women, does not have to mean defining a fixed category and policing it, but can mean, rather, a process of loving and valuing other women, and ourselves, and thus creating alternative women's identities. This only works, of course, if identifications are not necessarily locked into the binary of unity and closure—if identifications do not necessarily involve attempts to replace existential lack with delusions of unity and closure, but can involve desires for connection not based in lack, and in desire for closure, but in pleasure that opens and continues to open with each connection.[9] This means that our identifications open up the risk of pleasure as well as the necessity of conflict—both are risks of connection. It also means that practices of connection and identification open up to whomever might identify, however partially or contingently, weakly or strongly, as women, with various bodies, sexualities, orientations, and gender identities, and in various transitions. It is only through this opening up to transformative practices of connection and identification that the category "women" can be, in Butler's words, " a term in process, a becoming, a constructing that cannot rightfully be said to originate or to end" (Butler 1990, 33). We need to imagine and practice identifications with others that are not about establishing sameness (and that do not involve projection or incorporation) but that are about creating connection. When we do this an identity as a woman can be a home that is not a trap, but a source of freedom.

The argument for the redefinition and recreation of women through relations among women has opened up new horizons in many of our practices, and in some academic disciplines, for example in some women's history and literature. But in feminist theory we have been too often stuck between two poles: either the affirmation of a positive content or essence of women or a negation of any content—but this negation leaves us with only the man/woman binary, and with the constitution of women as subjected, which has itself been rigidified into a substantive definition.

I am arguing, then, that we can rethink women's identity as a practice of identifications—of new ways of saying "we." To do this, we need to rethink freedom, to understand these practices of identification as practices of freedom.

Feminism and the Abyss of Freedom

In her book, *Feminism and the Abyss of Freedom,* Linda Zerilli seems to open up just this possibility of the political re-creation of women through women's practices. "We have lost sight of the possibility that counterpractices of political association need not reproduce subjected identities as the condition of having anything political to say, but might create public spaces in which something is said that changes what can be heard as a political claim and also alters the context in which identities themselves are presently constituted as subject/ed. This possibility is related to the inaugural power of speech and action. Our ability to project a word such as *women* into new and unforeseen contexts is connected to the power of political association to create new (more freedom-affirming) attachments to the world and others" (Zerilli 2005, 23–4).

In her reading of the work of the Milan Women's Bookstore Collective, Zerilli argues that the collective provides an examplar of feminist community building as a practice of freedom. Drawing on Hannah Arendt, Zerilli argues that the Milanese feminists invite us to move out of the focus on the metaphysical question of identity, and into feminist practices of freedom. The Milan feminists, she argues, are engaged in a practice of world-building, through the free practice of relations among women, and through the creation of public spaces in which free relations among women can take shape.

For me, this work offers the possibility of a shift from a metaphysical to a practical and relational and *political* conception of identity. Specifically, it opens up the possibility that women's identity is being constituted—re-created—through these practices of freedom, through the creation of new kinds of intersubjective relations among women.

But Zerilli backs away from this possibility. Understandably impatient with the identity wars, she argues that feminists need to move out of our preoccupation with what she calls "the subject question"—move out of our preoccupation with questions of individual and collective identity—into a feminism focused on practices of freedom. Thus, in spite of what she suggests in the passage quoted above, she frames her argument in terms of an opposition between questions of identity and practices of freedom which, I want to argue, is a false opposition, based on an unquestioned acceptance of the equation of identity with entrapment, and of subjects with subjugation.[10] I shall argue that we can draw on feminist practices of freedom not to provide an alternative to the subject question, but to rethink the question, and to remake ourselves as subjects—as women.

Zerilli, drawing on the Milan feminists, shares my apprehension regarding the strategy of self-negation as a feminist strategy. The Milanese feminists, Zerilli notes, reject the argument that women's emancipation can be attained only once women "commit suicide" as women.

> The idea that "those individuals who are today defined as women must eradicate their own definition…, in a sense, commit suicide," as Ti-Grace Atkinson once famously declared, is utterly foreign to the Italian women's project of freedom.
>
> If what is past is the condition of what is and thus of one's own existence, the wish to destroy can lead to what Nietzsche diagnosed as the self-loathing and enervating features of the impossible wish to will backwards. According to Nietzsche, the "It was" is crushing—for the past does not budge. The will's relationship to what is past is "I will and cannot." Because it can be neither forgotten nor changed, the past must be redeemed. To redeem the past one must alter one's relationship to it: "To redeem what is past and transform every 'It was' into 'Thus I would have it!'—that's what I take to be redemption."
>
> Like Nietzsche, the Italians hold that to redeem the past is to give oneself value, to create new values. But what would redemption look like in the context of a feminist practice of freedom, a politics of sexual difference? How might feminists affirm sexual difference without reinstating what Monique Wittig calls the "category of sex"? (Zerilli, 99)

I would argue that redeeming ourselves and our past would involve coming to recognize that we have been and are produced, as women, not just through relations of domination, but through intersubjective relations that affirm our value and empower us. And this means that "women"— both who we are and who we understand ourselves to be—are constituted through these practices of revaluing, and through recognizing the history of our practices of valuing ourselves as women. Redeeming ourselves, then, requires *practices of identification* that change who we are and thus change the meaning of "women."

Zerilli seems to suggest something like this when she describes the Milan collective's focus on resymbolizing sexual difference. For the Milanese feminists, she argues, the contingent fact of sexual difference is "not to be destroyed or transcended, but rather resymbolized, transformed 'from a social cause of unfreedom into the principle of our [women's] freedom'" (98, quoting SD 122). But for Zerilli, feminists must "affirm sexual difference without reinstating…'the category of sex'" (99). What can this mean? Zerilli notes that American readers of the work of the Milan collective have typically dismissed their arguments as a return to essentialism—to an affirmation of women's difference—but she argues that this reading has missed the point. The Milan feminists, she argues, have shifted from a feminism focused on the question of women's identity to a feminism focused on a practice of freedom—from a practice of questioning what we are to a practice of saying "we." "Thinking about women as a political collectivity, rather than a sociological group or social subject, means thinking the 'we' of feminism anew: as the fragile achievement of practices of freedom" (24).

The Subject Question and the Paradox of Freedom

To understand what she means by this we need to understand Zerilli's critique of "the subject question." Zerilli argues that feminists have been too preoccupied with questions about the formation of the subject and of its capacities (or lack thereof) for agency—for resistance and change. For Zerilli, the subject question includes both questions about individual subjects and their agency and questions about the category of women as the subject of feminism—questions of the identity of women. Zerilli argues that feminists need to follow Arendt in shifting the question of freedom outside its current subject-centered frame, as a way to escape "our current entanglement in the paradoxes of subject formation and the vicious circle of agency" (12). To avoid these paradoxes and entanglements, we need to shift to a focus on freedom that focuses on the "who"—the "unique disclosure of human action," in contrast to the "what"—the identity or substance (13). "Whereas feminists have focused on the question of whether political agency is possible in the absence of the 'what' (for example, an identity such as 'women'), Arendt insists that politics is not about the 'what' and agency, but always about the 'who' and nonsovereignty" (13). Thus, Zerilli, following Arendt, sets up an opposition between freedom, which is characterized by the free action of the "who," and identity, which is the substance or the "what." She argues, further, that feminist preoccupations with the subject and agency have tended to equate freedom with sovereignty: with a capacity to control the outcome of action. "The requirement of agency is entangled in an identification of freedom with sovereignty and an instrumental conception of politics which deny… plurality" (12–13). According to Arendt, freedom is action, is doing, which opens us to contingency: we cannot control the outcome of our actions. Feminists, Zerilli argues, need to shift from our introspective preoccupation with our subjectivity (the "what") and agency and step into what Arendt calls the "abyss of freedom"—to practice political freedom through practices of world-building.

Zerilli argues, then, that the Milanese feminists redeem the past—redeem sexual difference—through the free practice of affirming community with other women: in Beauvoir's words, of saying "we." And she argues that the Milanese collective's creation of feminist public spaces exemplifies Arendt's ideal of promising. Thus, Zerilli argues that for the Milan feminists, "feminist world-building requires the social inscription of sexual difference, not as a form of subjectivity but as a resolutely political practice of 'free relations among women.' These relations involve the articulation of a new social contract organized around not female identity (be it natural or social) but the willingness to make judgments and promises with other women in a public space" (29).

I welcome Zerilli's call for a shift from a preoccupation with the paradoxes of identity and agency into practices of freedom. I think that our focus on what blocks our resistance has often blinded us to the ways in which we do resist, and our tendency to see agency as absolute—as all-or-nothing—has often blinded us to the agency that we do have. And I think that we need to open up possibilities for action, for freedom, that depend less on knowing who (or what) we are, and more on saying "we." I want to argue, however, that these acts of freedom are re-creating our identities as women—are changing what and who women are. Rather than setting up an opposition between freedom and identity—between freedom as "who" we are, as spontaneity, action, doing, and identity as "what" we are, as fixed substance or thing—I want to argue that our actions constitute and reconstitute our identities, and that in turn those identities enable our actions. And thus our freedom is not opposed to our identity, but is crucial to the enactment of our identities. Our identities are the interrelation between who we are and what we are, who we understand ourselves to be and what we make of ourselves.

Thus while for Zerilli the "we" of feminism as a political collectivity is opposed to any "we" as a "sociological group or social subject," I want to argue that the former produces and transforms the latter, which in turn enables the former. While Zerilli sets up a strict duality or binary between political collectivity and social subject (between freedom and identity) and argues that freedom is possible only through opposing and escaping identity, I argue that practices of identification can be practices of freedom.

I think that Zerilli has turned to a strict separation between the subject question, on one hand, and practices of freedom on the other, because the dominant contemporary feminist theories of the subject have led us to an impasse. Once we accept that the subject is produced only through disciplinary regimes of subjectification, then the subject's struggles for freedom can only be paradoxical. Once we accept that women are constituted only through disciplinary regimes of gender identity, then any call for women's emancipation is paradoxical. Zerilli argues that to escape the paradox, we must escape the subject question. I think that the question will continue to haunt us until we change the way that we formulate it, and the ways that we answer it.

If the paradox of freedom emerges because we believe on one hand that the subject (or agent) is constituted through subjection and on the other hand that that agency must equal absolute control, then rather than arguing that we need to reject both subjects and agency, we need to rethink both of these. We need to reconceive subject identity as constituted through multiple relations, and we need to reconceive agency in the terms offered by Arendt and Zerilli for rethinking freedom: as open-ended and intersubjective, as opening into plurality. Oddly, rather than arguing for a different conception of agency as capacity for action—for the term "agent," after all, comes from the Latin *agere,* which means "do"—Zerilli argues for the rejection of theories of agency altogether.

Because she accepts the equation of agency with the fantasy of absolute control, and the equation of subject identity with subjection, with entrapment in unfreedom, Zerilli concludes that there is no way of answering the subject question and the question of freedom without becoming mired in paradox. Thus, for Zerilli, redeeming the past by practicing freedom requires escaping altogether the question of subject identity. "When read through the frame of the subject question," Zerilli writes, the Milanese feminists' call to redemption is just another entanglement in the paradox of freedom: in what Wendy Brown calls the "'paradoxical' entanglement of modern struggles for freedom, like feminism, in 'the very structure of oppression that freedom emerges to oppose'" (Zerilli, 99; quoting Brown, 7). Zerilli, then, accepts that the subject question inevitably returns us to this paradox. But in accepting this, Zerilli is accepting that the subject question is already answered by the pronouncement that the identity "women" is an effect of subjugation, and that freedom can be found only in escape from that identity. In fact, Zerilli is critical of Butler's and Brown's Derridean-Foucaultian accounts of the paradoxical character of subject formation, arguing that both Butler and Brown are still mired in the question of subject identity: rather than moving out of "the subject-centred frame" they merely move into "its negative space" (12). With this move, she argues, "it seems as if the paradox of subject formation is installed as a vicious circle of agency at the heart of politics" (12). But rather than suggesting that a different formulation of the subject question might provide more helpful directions, might help us get out of the vicious circle of agency and provide a better sense of who (not what) we are and of what we can do, Zerilli argues that we must leave the terrain of the subject question altogether.

Thus, it appears that Zerilli agrees with Butler and Brown that the identity "women" is an effect of subjection. And therefore that women are constituted through subjection. And therefore that feminism (like all democratic politics) is inevitably haunted by the "paradox of founding": "if feminine subjects are constituted as subjected, as feminists of all three waves in their different ways have held, how are they to engage in the free act of founding something new?" (168). Thus she agrees that women are constituted as subjected, and that political action requires that we escape this identity in order to create something new. Not by repudiating the category women, but by refusing to engage with the question of identity, and by moving into practices of freedom.

I agree that we need to create something new, but I want to suggest that instead of assuming that the subject question has already been answered, we need to rethink the question. Instead of escaping the subject question to move into practices of freedom, we need to understand our practices of freedom as changing the subject. Because Zerilli does not attempt to change the subject question, she leaves it mired in paradox.

The problem is that when we attempt to practice freedom, to say "we," we are not in fact able to escape our identities, but are dragging them along with us, with all of their paradoxes unresolved, blocking our action. Saying "we" without self-negation requires creating new psychic attachments and identifications with ourselves and each other—attachments that open up conflict and wounds, but that also offer the possibility of healing those wounds. It also requires the development of a sense of ourselves, as women, that can enable further action: a conviction that being a woman can mean something other than being subjected.

The Category of Women

Again, this is a possibility that Zerilli seems to open up only to close off once more. Zerilli notes that the critique of the category "women" has been wrongly interpreted as a skeptical claim about the existence of women. She points out that the critique of the category, in the work of Judith Butler and others, should be taken not as an expression of radical doubt—"are there women really?"— but as the recognition that the practice of feminism can no longer rest on a coherent foundational category of women. For Zerilli, this means that the way is open for us to practice feminism anew: once we understand feminist theory not as an epistemological enterprise based on skepticism about knowledge claims, and on the production of new knowledge claims, but as an act of imagination, then feminist theory can support feminism as a political practice of free political action and association. Drawing on Wittgenstein, Cavell, and Castoriadis, Zerilli argues that feminist practice requires not a certainty about the subject of women, but doing—transforming, world-building, beginning anew. This requires a reconceptualization of theory as an act of imagination, as "the creation of new figures of the thinkable."[11] For Zerilli, the most insightful, creative, and radical achievement of Judith Butler's *Gender Trouble* is its generation of "a figure of the newly thinkable" in the account of drag as subversive. Butler reworks the drag performance of femininity in such a way that it allows her to "think gender anew" (61). Unfortunately, Zerilli argues, Butler becomes entangled in the very skeptical problematic she sets out to challenge. Arguing that it is "only from a self-consciously denaturalized position" that we can see how the appearance of naturalness of the two-sex model of gender is constituted,[12] Butler falls back on the assumption that problematizing gender requires a Cartesian act of radical doubt, detaching from everything that we have assumed, to engage in an interpretive act that will produce new, true knowledge. Drawing on Wittgenstein and Cavell, Zerilli argues that changes in the meaning of gender "emerge not through the skeptical insight that gender as such is contingent and can therefore be changed (for example, we have the theory, now we can act), but through the projection of a word like *women* into a new context, where it is taken up by others in ways we can neither predict nor control" (65). Thus, the constitution of gender in language is not the trap that Butler believes it to be: language is not a closed system that depends on the uniform application of a rule or law, but a process in which words take on new meanings in different contexts. Thus, we do not have to rely on failure to cite norms properly in order to change meanings. Questioning norms depends on access to other norms, and changes in meaning depend on subjective and collective judgments made in particular contexts. "Following Wittgenstein, we do not need to posit failure as an internal condition of language to stave off meaning determinism because the successful application of concepts does not carry with it the threat of closure of meaning that Butler, following Derrida, seems to assume. Language is not a cage from which only the essential possibility of failure in language can save us" (53). Thus, feminists' capacity to change the conditions in which we find ourselves rests on "the factical character of human freedom, the capacity to wrest something new from an objective state of affairs without being compelled to do so by a norm or rule" (65).

I am persuaded by Zerilli's argument that what feminism and feminist theory need are practices of freedom, and that what Butler offers is the "disturbing" figure of drag that allows us to reimagine gender. And I agree with Zerilli's Wittgensteinian argument that the meanings of words like "women" are not fixed but change in context, and that we therefore have a measure of freedom to create something new.[13] I think that this means that we have some freedom to constitute the meanings of our gender identities, and that this freedom goes beyond the "freedom" to fail to cite norms properly—the freedom borne of compulsion—and beyond the freedom to cite norms subversively. I also agree that we do not have complete control over this process or its results. If we accept Wittgenstein's argument that language is not a cage but allows for different meanings that change with contexts—that meanings are context-dependent— then the implication is that identities like women are different in different contexts (and this is the argument that Cressida Heyes has made). It also means that identities like women can change and be transformed through women's practices. And that's what Zerilli seems to suggest when she writes that changes in the meaning of gender emerge through "the projection of a word like *women* into a new context, where it is taken up by others in ways we can neither predict nor control" (65). But having suggested this, Zerilli falls back into familiar oppositions. Zerilli takes Wittgenstein's argument to mean that when we use language, we are engaging in a doing, not a knowing. Drawing on Arendt, Zerilli draws the conclusion, for feminists, that: "We simply cannot know what we do, at least not in the ways required by a means-ends conception of politics" (64). "A freedom-centred feminism, after all, is concerned not with knowing (that there are women) as such, but with doing—with transforming, world-building, beginning anew" (65). Thus, Zerilli repeats the opposition between freedom and identity, now dependent on an opposition between doing and knowing that is too stark and simplistic. Having criticized Butler for taking up the role of the skeptic, and thus failing to escape a preoccupation with knowledge as certainty, with knowing fixed and unassailable truths, Zerilli only repeats this conception of knowledge, and argues that we must escape it. As Linda Alcoff has argued, this conception of knowledge is outdated: contemporary epistemology has moved beyond the metaphysics of substance and the epistemology of certainty to more fluid conceptions of knowledge.[14] I think we can draw on Wittgenstein not to escape from knowledge into doing, but to develop a different form of knowledge. Rather than doing without knowing, we need a different, more pragmatic understanding of knowing, a knowing that is a doing, or that is much more closely related to doing. I would argue that rather than romanticizing headless doing, spontaneous expression, feminists need an enabling sense of who we are and what we can do. What we do helps to build that sense of ourselves, but our doing is also dependent on our sense of ourselves as agents with capacities for action. And this is why "the subject question" still matters.

Zerilli argues that we need a feminism based on "the faculty of presentation (imagination) and the creation of figures of the newly thinkable rather than the faculty of concepts (understanding) and the ability to subsume particulars under rules" (64). Thus, she writes, "Emphasizing imagination, rather than understanding and reason, as crucial to such judgment and as the political faculty par excellence, Arendt helps us understand why the collapse of the category of women need by no means spell the end of feminism, for a freedom-centred feminism never relied on concept-application in the first place" (30). Here Zerilli opposes imagination to reason—another false opposition—reducing understanding to a subsuming of particulars under rules or concepts, and reduces the category of women to a concept that must be applied. But as Zerilli herself has noted, a term like "women" is *not* a fixed concept that we apply. Wittgenstein's point was that the term or category changes in context, according to use. And if, as Zerilli writes, "political claims" depend not on their being epistemologically justified but on being "taken up by others" (30) then the collapse of the category may well spell the end of feminism. Because what is at stake is not epistemological justification. What is at stake is our capacity to *identify with* each other and with ourselves as women—with whom and what we are. What is at stake, moreover, is our capacity to identify with the "political claims" that we are making: with issues and goals that are specific to struggles for women's freedom. For freedom is not, after all, just action, but is also action directed by particular human beings toward specific problems and goals.

Recognition, Identity, and Freedom

This opens up the fraught question of the politics of recognition and reparation, and their relation to identities and to freedom. With Wendy Brown, Zerilli argues that struggles for recognition keep us stuck in our identities, mired in *ressentiment*, demanding recognition and reparation that we will never, ever receive. The Milan Collective, she writes, agrees that the demand for reparation only reinstalls injury as identity, and thus precludes our freedom. "Claims for reparation leave the past unredeemed, entrapping women in an endless pursuit of social recognition of their pain, which, in turn, only further constitutes 'women' as an injury identity" (100). Thus, we need to shift our focus from claims for recognition, reparations, and rights, to creative practices of freedom.

Brown's argument rests on the claim that "politicized identity" becomes attached to its own exclusion "because it is premised on this exclusion for its very existence as identity" (Brown, 73–4). I have argued that this understanding of politicized identity is far too narrow: it recognizes only one dimension of identity and excludes all others. Zerilli argues, following the Milan Collective, that since women do not actually identify with the victim identity, but project it onto other women, "the 'wounded attachment' Brown speaks of looks rather like an injury identity inhabited by none *and* 'a mass identification with the suffering of some.'"[15] While feminism is trapped in the logic of reparation by an injury identity, this is not an identity that is shared by all, but is the only figure around which we can mobilize politically in the absence of a "figure of female freedom" (Zerilli, 102). What is needed, then, is a "figure of female freedom" to counteract the "injury identity." "For a woman, then, the only way out of the apparent impasse of the logic of reparation or woundedness as the condition of modern political subjectivity described by Wendy Brown is to acknowledge what one owes to other women, to acknowledge, that is, community" (116).

> The politics of sexual difference as the Italians understand it, then, would transform the I-will that remains bound to necessity, caught in a fantasy of self-sovereignty, and filled with *ressentiment,* into the I-can that experiences freedom in a community at once conditioned and chosen: "a social contract…based on the principle of gratitude and exchange with other women" (SD, 142). This new social contract is based not on a set of rationally agreed upon principles…but on a *promise* to make good a claim to community and acknowledge a debt. (117)

The Milan feminists argue that feminist freedom consists not in struggles for recognition or rights, but in developing a political and personal accountability to women. Feminist freedom is "the capacity to found new forms of political association" (98).

I think that Zerilli is absolutely right to argue that feminists need to move out of the impasse of the logic of woundedness, and into practices of freedom in community, and in political association. For me, this means that we can open our understanding of our identity as women to include not just an injury identity but an identity forged through relations among women, and an identity forged through saying "we" as agents of practices of freedom.

But the simple opposition between demands for rights and reparations, based on the demand for recognition of identity that mires us in our victimhood, on the one hand, and practices of freedom, on the other, does not allow for the possibility that practices of freedom might include re-creations of our identities, and therefore of the kinds of recognition we might be looking for. This account assumes that claims for recognition and reparation are always based on claims of fixed identity categories, and that these identities are always victim identities. Thus, claims for recognition inevitably entrap us in the paradox of identity, which renders the claims unrealizable. This account, then, does not allow for the possibility that women might be recognized as complex and changing identities. It does not allow, moreover, for the possibility that some of our demands might be met, because some of our claims might be recognized as valid; and that this might lead not to fixing but to changing our identities. Finally, this account assumes that we can never move beyond an "us vs. them" model of recognition. In fact, struggles for recognition are more complicated: we seek recognition not just from "our oppressors" but from each other, and we are all implicated in the relations of recognition and power that subject and enable us.

Zerilli does argue that rather than simply rejecting rights for freedom, we need to rethink rights claims as practices of freedom: "a claim to rights is not—or not simply—a demand for recognition of *what* one is; it is a demand for acknowledgment of *who* one is, and, more important, of who one might *become*" (121). Here she suggests that rights claims can open up a space of freedom rather than locking us into fixed identities; yet she maintains the equation of struggles for recognition with entrapment in identities (we can be recognized only for *what* we are) and argues that rights claims can move beyond struggles for recognition insofar as we are acknowledged as free actors projecting possible futures. This distinction turns on her understanding of recognition as being caught in the logic of knowledge, while acknowledgement goes beyond knowledge to action.[16] But if we look at the history of feminist struggles for recognition, we will see that these struggles do not fix but transform women's identities. As I argued in chapter 3, our theoretical and practical engagements in these struggles have required us to confront differences and conflicts among women, and among systems and structures of oppression, so that our understandings of who and what we are struggling for have opened up, to become much more complex and diverse. And struggles for recognition have often served to transform who we are, from victims to agents of change: for example, from household servants and housewives to workers, from enslaved and disenfranchised to political participants, from nonpersons to persons, from deviant to proudly queer, from unintelligible to intelligible.

Thus, the identity "women" is an identity in process—is being re-created in part by feminists engaged in practices of identity-building, as well as world-building. And one of these practices is feminist solidarity. While Zerilli makes a strong case for the creation of feminist public spaces, for the importance of feminist community, which involves a practice of saying "we," and promising, she never uses the term "solidarity." I think this may be because solidarity is precisely resistance to oppression: in Amy Allen's words, "solidarity is the ability of a collectivity to act together for the agreed-upon end of challenging, subverting, and, ultimately, overturning a system of domination" (Allen, 127). For Zerilli, and for the Milan feminists, as for Wendy Brown, this understanding of collectivity just returns us to the paradox of demands for recognition and reparation. But as Allen argues, feminist politics must be rooted in a form of power that is stronger than the "power-with" that Arendt argues for. If we are to understand promise-keeping as something more than "honour among thieves," we need to affirm feminist solidarity as a collective resistance to oppression, sustained by interactions characterized by reciprocity and mutuality. This means that we need to include resistance to oppression in our understanding of freedom.

Another reason for avoiding the term "solidarity" would be the sense that this term implies a false unity, and does not allow for plurality and difference. Zerilli argues that the Milan feminists are held together "only by an agreed purpose for which alone the promises are valid and binding."[17] But while the argument that feminists are held together by an agreed purpose avoids miring feminists in a substantive subject identity, or category, the claim that we are held together *only* by a shared purpose, and only in a particular public realm, reduces our solidarity to a depthless voluntarism, emptied of motivation, of affect, or shared experience, and, moreover, renders our practices and associations outside of this realm empty of political import.

In chapter 3, I argue that feminist solidarity plays, and has always played, an important role in constituting women's identity. Moreover, I think that essential to solidarity are practices of *identification*: identification with ideals, with women as a "we," and with each other. Thus, the practice of saying "we" grows out of and produces subjective identifications, rooted in diverse histories and practices, and not just public feminist spaces. And these feminist practices of identification are changing the meaning of "women" for all who identify as women, and not just for members of feminist political groups.

Feminism and Freedom

The central argument of *Feminism and the Abyss of Freedom* is that feminist freedom should not be a means to an end, but should be an end in itself. Of course, this opens up the question as to what exactly freedom is. And there have been many answers to that question. Freedom has been understood to be the absence of oppression, and the absence of interference. It has been defined as self-ownership, self-realization, and self-expression. It has been located in the public realm and in the private realm and in the mind. Freedom has been defined as the capacity to participate in the collective life of a society, and as the condition of being in nonalienated relationships of interdependence, and as capacities for critique, agency, and change. Freedom, then, can mean a lot of different things. For Zerilli, following Arendt, freedom is action, is beginning anew. More specifically, freedom is acting and interacting with others in public space, engaging in projects of world-building. To be free is to act, and action necessarily brings us into the sphere of human plurality. Arendt argues that in the Western tradition, freedom is equated with sovereignty, and plurality has been seen to be a weakness, "at best an indication of our unfortunate dependence on others, which we should strive to overcome" (Zerilli, 16). Thus we need to reject the conception of freedom as sovereignty, as self-sufficiency and mastery, and recognize that dependence on others is a condition of freedom, that freedom requires community, and this opens up the reality of plurality. It is our dependence on others, then, that produces "inherent unpredictability" and "irreducible contingency" (24). Thus, action's "tremendous capacity for establishing relationships" is inseparable from its "inherent unpredictability" and "boundlessness."[18] Action opens into the "abyss of freedom" in all of its "frightening arbitrariness" (25).

Zerilli's Arendtian argument is important: she reconceives feminist freedom as freedom in community, in dependence on others, and in relations of plurality and diversity. Yet, while it is certainly true that freedom does open up uncertainty and contingency, and this is an important corrective to ideals of mastery, the representation of freedom as an abyss of uncertainty is a little too reminiscent of the American frontier, and of the independent individual who confronts it. In replacing the ideal of sovereignty with the image of the abyss, with "inherent unpredictability," "irreducible contingency," and "frightening arbitrariness" Zerilli, following Arendt, is doing what she has criticized Butler for doing: moving into the "negative space" of the subject-centered frame. Freedom now is not sovereignty but radical contingency. And perhaps this is just another way of expressing the fear of dependence on others.[19]

To be free is to act—yes. But this doesn't mean leaping into the unknown; it means opening up to otherness, to others, who are not an abyss but other people. To see freedom as action opening into an abyss is to see freedom as action without an addressee. Thus we remain within a subject-centered frame, with the atomistic individual acting into an abyss. Surely it is more accurate to see freedom as intersubjective and interdependent: we act not into an abyss but toward others, toward concrete people and places in the world, toward ideals and dreams and desires, and toward ourselves as well. And we depend on others, on our bodies, on the world. When I act, I depend on the ground beneath my feet, and I depend on my feet. The ground may open up, my feet may stumble, and I may have to find a different way. When we speak, we depend on our voices, and we depend on others to listen. Our voices may break, and others may not listen or understand. We cannot know what they will do, and we cannot know what will happen. We may find that we need to do a lot more listening than speaking. But we will not find ourselves in an abyss. We will find ourselves dependent on others.

Thus, while freedom involves beginning anew, opening up to uncertainty and contingency, it also involves creating new connections, new homes. I prefer to understand freedom not as hurling oneself into an abyss, but as risking connection. Not as leaping into the unknown, but as risking dependence on others, and on the world, to create something new. For women, then, freedom involves the capacity to transform who and what we are, so that we can become more at home in our relations with each other, ourselves, and the world. Freedom, then, involves transforming women.

In the next chapter, I ask whether this understanding of freedom in connection can help us to cross borders between cultures and convictions, to rethink the agency of women in a religious and "illiberal" tradition, and to rethink the liberal grounds of feminism.

Notes

1. See Toril Moi's important book, *What is a Woman?* Moi's first chapter is "an attempt to liberate the word 'woman' from the binary straitjacket that contemporary sex and gender theory imprisons it in" (Moi 1999, ix). Drawing on Beauvoir's understanding of "the body in situation" and Wittgenstein's understanding of concepts in language, Moi argues for "a feminist theory that starts from an ordinary understanding of what a woman is, namely a person with a female body" (8). Arguing that "What we need today more than ever is a feminism committed to seeking justice and equality for women, in the most ordinary sense of the word" (9). Moi develops an anti-essentialist, non-metaphysical theory of subjectivity and of the body. She stresses, however, that this is not a theory of identity, which she calls "an exhausted category" (viii).

2. Toril Moi argues that such arguments misread Beauvoir and are predicated on a problematic sex/gender distinction. See Moi 1999. See also Gatens 1996, Heinämaa 2003, Kruks 2001).

3. I develop this argument at length in *Sacrificial Logics.*

4. Atkinson, 49, as quoted by Zerilli, 14.

5. Here I am referring to Alcoff, "The Metaphysics of Gender and Sexual Difference," in *Visible Identities.* Alcoff develops a complex philosophical account of relational identities that goes far beyond the extent of my argument here, as well as trenchant critiques of political and philosophical critiques of identity, in the earlier chapters of *Visible Identities.* See also Paula Moya's complex realist understanding of identities in terms of multiple relations. Some important feminist work focuses on rethinking the relation between sex and gender, rethinking the role of embodiment, and rethinking the materiality of the sexed body. See, for example, Gatens 1996, Grosz 1994, Moi 1999, and work in the "new materialisms"—for example, Coole and Frost 2010.

6. Here Butler makes this argument by differentiating the "term" women from an "identity" women, where the former is the referent and the latter is a content that is signified. She argues that the referent can be distinguished from the signified content and thus "released into a future of multiple significations." But in most of her discussions of identity, Butler argues that identity is precisely a linguistic category.

7. Basic texts include Fausto-Sterling (1992, 2000), Sedgwick (1990), Feinberg (1992), Stryker and Whittle (2006).

8. Prosser, 73, quoting Thompson. My emphasis.

9. Here I am thinking of the work of Luce Irigaray.

10. This opposition appears in other important feminist attempts to rethink freedom from a Foucaultian perspective. See, for example, McWhorter 2004.

11. Zerilli, 63: quoting Castoriadis, 269–71.

12. Zerilli, 48; quoting Butler, *Gender Trouble,* 110.

13. For this argument see also Nicholson 1994, Heyes 2000, and Medina 2003. I refer to this argument in *Sacrificial Logics*, 121.
14. Alcoff, "The Metaphysics of Gender and Sexual Difference," in *Visible Identities*.
15. Zerilli, 101; quoting the Milan Collective, 102.
16. Zerilli takes the distinction between knowledge and acknowledgement from Cavell.
17. Zerilli, 118; quoting Arendt.
18. Zerilli, 24, quoting Arendt, *The Human Condition*, 191.
19. The conception of freedom as action opening into an abyss echoes the existentialist understanding of freedom as transcendence of what is—i.e., as negativity vs. identity. I discuss this conception of freedom and its influence on feminist and poststructuralist critiques of identity in the first chapter of *Sacrificial Logics*.

5 FEMINISM AND THE ISLAMIC REVIVAL: FREEDOM AS A PRACTICE OF BELONGING

For our part, we hold that the only public good is that which assures the private good of the citizens.... But we do not confuse the idea of private interest with that of happiness ... Are not women of the harem more happy than women voters? Is not the housekeeper happier than the working-woman? ...

Every subject plays his part as such specifically through exploits or projects that serve as a mode of transcendence; he achieves liberty only through a continual reaching out towards other liberties. There is no justification for present existence other than its expansion into an indefinitely open future.

SIMONE DE BEAUVOIR, *THE SECOND SEX*

How do we conceive of individual freedom in a context where the distinction between the subject's own desires and socially prescribed performances cannot be easily presumed, and where submission to certain forms of (external) authority is a condition for achieving the subject's potentiality?

SABA MAHMOOD, *POLITICS OF PIETY*

Over the past couple of decades, issues of cultural difference have moved from the margins to the center of feminist theory. These issues problematize any simple answers to questions of equality or freedom for women, for such questions must address the reality that we are all embedded in and attached to specific cultural identities, within which we value different ways of flourishing; and they must confront the possibility that feminism itself may be wedded to particular cultural identities. In recent years the focus of discussions of cultural difference has shifted to religion, and in particular to the role of women in Islam. A great deal of work has addressed controversies around the veil, reflecting or confronting western anxieties about the Islamic revival. As Lila Abu-Lughod notes in the provocatively titled "Do Muslim Women Really Need Saving?" the American invasion of Afghanistan, like many colonial regimes, was repeatedly justified by the need to liberate women from the oppression of Muslim culture.[1] Such arguments place feminists in the company of strange bedfellows, indeed.

While some feminists, with other liberal and leftist theorists, argue that the recognition of cultural identities conflicts with the recognition of individual freedom and women's equality, others have argued against a simplistic and reductive response to cultural difference.[2] Uma Narayan criticizes both gender essentialism and cultural essentialism, arguing for a more complex understanding and analysis of the power relations in and between cultures.[3] Feminist critiques of the centrality of patriarchy in western culture remind us that all cultures and societies are founded on structures of inequality and oppression. Conversely, many theorists argue that ideals of freedom and equality can be found in all cultures—that these are genuinely universal ideals.[4]

At the same time, feminist critiques of western imperialism, colonialism, and racism, along with the challenge of cultural differences, might lead us to ask whether western feminists need to question our own assumptions about freedom and subordination. If there are different ways of flourishing, are there also different ways of being free? This is the question that frames this chapter.

Freedom in Subordination?

This question came up in an introductory class in women and gender studies, during a discussion of the argument that femininity is a form of subordination. A student who rarely spoke raised her hand and asked, hesitantly, whether it wasn't possible to be subordinate but still equal and still free? The question was intriguing: not least because it came in the middle of a fairly heated discussion as to whether subordination was symbolized more by veils and burqas, or by push-up bras and thongs, in a class in which many women wore veils, and many others were displaying cleavage. The question was asking, then, whether it wasn't possible to conform to various conventions and disciplines of femininity, and, even if these do symbolize and produce subordination, still be somehow equal and free?

Of course there is a simple answer: subordination and freedom are simply opposed. The question is simply an expression of confusion, a failure to accept a simple contradiction. As Simone de Beauvoir argued, we need to distinguish between freedom and happiness: a housewife may be happy, as might a woman in a harem, but neither is free. For Beauvoir, freedom requires resistance to conventions, transcendence of given identities, regardless of whether or not these conventions and these identities might make us happy (and of course it must be stressed that very often they do not). Beauvoir is admirably clear about this, and her contempt for happiness is palpable: a squirrel can be happy; a human being strives toward freedom. And the drama of woman inheres in the contradiction she lives, between aspiring to be a free subject, and being condemned to conform to the conventions of the second sex.

Feminists are habituated to living within a sharp contrast between the real and the ideal: between the ideals of freedom and justice and equality, and the reality of subordination. One way that feminist theorists have addressed this binary between the real and the ideal is to draw on conceptions of agency and freedom that move beyond the opposition between freedom and subordination, and the narrative of revolution, based on an opposition between the dystopic present and the utopian future. In the work of theorists like Michel Foucault and Hannah Arendt we find conceptions of freedom in capacities for agency that are constituted through relations of power that are inevitable in any human society. So, for Judith Butler, following Foucault, agency is enabled by the very operations of power that produce our subordination, and freedom is performed through acts of subversion of given norms. And for Linda Zerilli, following Arendt, we enact our freedom through our participation in the public world. For feminism, this doesn't mean that we necessarily give up the project of social transformation toward ideals of justice, equality, and liberation; it means that we engage in this project with a kind of radical acceptance of what is, and shift from a binary opposition between real and ideal to a recognition of freedoms being enacted in the present: from "another world is possible" to "another world is actual."[5] Thus we become able to recognize the diversity of practices of freedom that are already in play, rather than living in wounded attachment to our victimhood.[6] This allows us, analytically, to shift from a totalizing critique that induces paralysis to a critical analysis focused on concrete possibilities for transformation; and practically, to shift from an experience of futility and impotence in the face of the enormity of global injustice, to a capacity to value acts of freedom for themselves and for their relation to a community of freedom and resistance. So, rather than accept the simple contradiction between subordination and freedom, we can find that we do have freedom within our relations of subordination.

The Islamic Revival and the Feminist Subject

In her book, *Politics of Piety*, Saba Mahmood analyzes the contemporary women's piety movement in the mosques of Cairo, Egypt, to consider the meaning of agency when subordination to external authority is the condition for the development of the self. Mahmood's book is based on her ethnographic study of the piety movement, or mosque movement, which is part of the Islamic revival of the past few decades. According to participants, this movement has "emerged in response to the perception that religious knowledge, as a means of organizing daily conduct, had become increasingly marginalized under modern structures of secular governance." The perception is that Islamic knowledge had been "reduced to an abstract system of beliefs with no direct bearing on the practicalities of daily living" (Mahmood 2005, 4). So the piety movement is focused on bringing religious principles into daily life.

Mahmood herself is an outsider in this investigation. A longtime secular leftist and feminist, Mahmood focuses on the challenge posed by the piety movement to her own feminist values and beliefs: the subtitle of the book is *The Islamic Revival and the Feminist Subject*. For Mahmood, the piety movement "poses a dilemma for feminist analysts. On the one hand, the women in this movement are asserting their presence in previously male-defined spheres," (4) gathering in mosques to teach Islamic doctrine to each other, and thereby "altering the historically male-centred character of mosques as well as Islamic pedagogy" (2). On the other hand, "the very idioms they use to enter these arenas are grounded in discourses that have historically secured their subordination to male authority. In other words, women's subordination to feminine virtues, such as shyness, modesty, and humility, appears to be the necessary condition for their enhanced public role in religious and political life" (5–6).[7] Moreover, while the piety movement stresses the responsibility of each individual to study and interpret the conflicting interpretations of religious doctrine, and while each woman has made the choice herself to engage in this study, often against the wishes of husbands and other family members, the goal of the practice is to discover and adhere as closely as possible to the authority of that doctrine.

For Mahmood, the study of the piety movement raises crucial questions about the normative liberal assumptions that underlie feminism: in particular, the feminist allegiance to an unquestioned ideal of individual freedom. Mahmood argues that we need to question this dogma, to detach conceptions of self-realization and of agency from the ideal of freedom, to question the assumption that agency necessarily involves the desire for autonomy and the ability to resist and subvert norms. She argues, then, for a conception of agency entailed "not only in those acts that resist norms but also in the multiple ways in which one *inhabits* norms" (15). Mahmood is arguing, then, that we need to see the women in the piety movement as agents engaged in practices of self-realization that we westerners—and we feminists—can recognize as good lives, even though they conflict with our ideals of freedom. Moreover, they provoke us to question our own ideals, to ask whether the ideal of freedom is in fact a dogmatic ideal.

Mahmood argues that not just liberal but also poststructuralist feminisms invoke an unquestioned ideal of freedom: she notes that Judith Butler and other poststructuralist theorists conceive of agency only within the binary terms of conformity or resistance to norms, such that agency is always understood as resistance to or subversion of norms. Thus, "the normative political subject of poststructuralist theory often remains a liberatory one, whose agency is conceptualized on the binary model of subordination and subversion" (14).

I agree with the critique of this binary—of the idea that agency must always be conceived in opposition to norms. As I have argued, social identities are not only effects of power but are our connections to each other and to ourselves, and so we need not only to question these identities and the norms they entail, but to find ways of inhabiting them differently. But I am reluctant to give up the aspiration to liberation. When Mahmood argues that feminists need to question the ideal of freedom, I wonder what else feminism could be about? Isn't feminism a movement to resist oppression, and to struggle for freedom? Perhaps we can shift our focus to the achievement of good lives for women, and that might be enough. But I would like to hold onto the aspiration to freedom. In this chapter, I would like to explore the possibility that there are different conceptions of freedom, and that Mahmood's study of the women in the mosque movement might help us to open up our understanding of what freedom might be.

Mahmood herself seems to be ambivalent on this point. While she asks us to question the assumption that agency must entail a struggle for freedom, at one point she suggests that the pietists offer "contrasting conceptions" and "different imaginaries" of personal and collective freedom, presupposing "different relations to forms of social authority" (122). She also asks, in a couple of places, how we might draw on the analysis of the women in the mosque movement to reconceptualize freedom: "How do we conceive of individual freedom in a context where the distinction between the subject's own desires and socially prescribed performances cannot be easily presumed, and where submission to certain forms of (external) authority is a condition for achieving the subject's potentiality?" (31).[8] The question is left hanging in the air, though answers are implied in Mahmood's analyses.

In this chapter, I shall take up this question, to ask whether Mahmood's analysis of the agency of the pietists can contribute to a feminist reconceptualization of freedom. I shall argue, first, that Mahmood is unable to address this question because of the limitations of the "paradox of subjectivation" model within which she locates the question of agency, and the limitations of the liberal model within which she frames the question of freedom. I think that

Mahmood does not pursue this question because she herself tends to accept an understanding of freedom as resistance to constraints, and hence to social norms. Thus, she defines agency as distinct from practices of freedom. I argue that the practices of the pietists can be understood through another understanding of agency, and of freedom: freedom as a practice of belonging. I take up four conceptions of freedom that emerge from Mahmood's analysis, to draw out this alternative conception of freedom as a practice of belonging.

The Paradox of Subjectivation

As I have noted, Mahmood argues that in order to understand the women in the mosque movement as agents, we need to understand agency not only in terms of resistance to norms, but also in terms of the variety of ways in which we inhabit norms. "I want to move away from an agonistic and dualistic framework—one in which norms are conceptualized on the model of doing and undoing, consolidation and subversion—and instead think about the variety of ways in which norms are lived and inhabited, aspired to reached for, and consummated" (23). Mahmood takes Foucault's late work on the ethics of the self as the theoretical framework for her analysis of the agency of the women in the mosque movement.

> I find Foucault's analysis of ethical formation particularly helpful for conceptualizing agency beyond the confines of the binary model of enacting and subverting norms. Specifically, he draws our attention to the contribution of external forms to the development of human ethical capacities, to specific modes of human agency. Instead of limiting agency to those acts that disrupt existing power relations, Foucault's work encourages us to think of agency: (a) in terms of the capacities and skills required to undertake particular kinds of moral actions; and (b) as ineluctably bound up with the historically and culturally specific disciplines through which a subject is formed. The paradox of subjectivation is central to Foucault's formulation in that the capacity of action is enabled and created by specific relations of subordination. To clarify this paradox, we might consider the example of a virtuoso pianist who submits herself to the often painful regime of disciplinary practice, as well as to the hierarchical structures of apprenticeship, in order to acquire the ability—the requisite agency—to play the instrument with mastery. Importantly, her agency is predicated upon her ability to be taught, a condition classically referred to as "docility." Although we

have come to associate docility with the abandonment of agency, the term literally implies the malleability required of someone in order for her to be instructed in a particular skill or knowledge—a meaning that carries less a sense of passivity than one of struggle, effort, exertion, and achievement. (29)

With the example of the virtuoso pianist, Mahmood is suggesting that the pietists' submission to authority, and to the disciplines required in order to achieve a certain ideal, or telos, is not so different from any form of discipline that we follow in order to achieve an ideal. The capacity to be taught—the capacity to learn through submission to particular disciplines—is central to the development of agency. Mahmood offers the example of the student learning to play piano to show that "submission to authority is a condition for achieving the subject's potentiality" (31). And surely this is the case for many of our practices that lead toward realizing an ideal: in order to become a doctor or a mechanic or a surfer or a cheerleader, one needs to accept the authority of the teacher, to learn the rules and practice the disciplines of one's craft—while also developing one's own original interpretations and techniques. We can go further to note that in order to become any kind of an agent, one needs to be socialized within a particular culture with its particular meanings and disciplines and practices.

The question is, why is this a paradox? It's a paradox only if we accept the very model of agency that Mahmood wants to criticize: the idea that our agency entails our capacity to resist norms; to resist any authority but our own. The fact that an agency understood as resistance to norms requires submission to authority is clearly paradoxical. For liberal individuals, the paradox is that our freedom, defined as absence of interference by others, rests on accepting social norms that are given not by ourselves but by others. For theorists of freedom as autonomy, the paradox is that our capacity for individual freedom, which rests on our capacity to access our true desires, or to act according to our own rational will, is secured through inhabiting norms that originate outside ourselves. Thus, it seems that Mahmood's acceptance of the paradox of subjectivation as a model of agency rests on an acceptance of a liberal model of freedom.

The development of agency through learning from a teacher and following particular disciplines is paradoxical only if we assume that learning and following are forms of oppressive subordination, and an understanding of agency as inhabiting norms is paradoxical only if we assume that social norms and social conventions are necessarily oppressive, and hence opposed to freedom: the paradox is that they are both oppressive and enabling. But surely not all norms and conventions are forces of oppressive subordination, and thus inhabiting norms is not necessarily a practice of oppressive subordination. Surely we would not want to say that the pianist, for example, is oppressed. The problem is that the paradigm of the paradox of subjectivation fails to distinguish between social norms and oppressive subordination, and rests on the assumption that all social norms are oppressive, or sources of subjugation. Thus, it rests on the assumption that freedom is necessarily resistance to social norms.

The paradox of subjectivation is very helpful in understanding the operations of power through which we are produced as subjects who practice, and desire, our own oppression; and in understanding how the agency produced through this process is the very agency required for resistance. The paradox, then, is that our agency, and our freedom, are produced through processes that secure our oppression. Feminists have long recognized that one reason for the intransigence of patriarchy is that we learn, as women, to want it: we want, for example, to care for others, to put care for others before ourselves, to smile, to look pretty, to be good mothers and wives and sex objects. What Foucault and Butler and feminist psychoanalytic theorists add to this recognition is that the processes that secure our oppression are the very processes that create a self, and enable our agency. So the process of acquiring an identity as a gendered self—as a woman—is the process of learning to want our subordination. Thus, the paradox of subjectivation can, from a feminist perspective, help us to understand how the women in the mosque movement practice their submission to patriarchal norms, and how this practice of submission simultaneously enables them as agents. But it does not provide an adequate account of the agency of the pietists from their own perspective: as Mahmood argues, for the pietists, their agency is *not* a practice of resistance to norms, and *not* a struggle for individual freedom from social constraints, but is a practice of enacting the will of God. And the pietists do not consider their submission to God's will to be in any way oppressive.

Moreover, as I shall argue, an understanding of the pietists' agency as an effect of subordination to God (or to social conventions or to authority) misses a central focus of their practices: the development of connection and closeness to God. The paradox of subjectivation model considers human relations to be relations of subordination and resistance. Thus, it provides an insightful account of "agency as a capacity for action that specific relations of *subordination* create and enable" (Mahmood,18; italics in original). But it cannot account for the ways in which agency is produced through inhabiting norms and social conventions that are not oppressive, and it cannot account for the development of agency through relations that are not relations of power, including relations of mutuality, care, and love.[9]

Thus, the paradigm of the paradox of subjectivation cannot fully account for the pietists' agency because, first, it equates agency with resistance, and second, it equates following a teacher or social conventions—inhabiting norms—with subordination. So long as we remain within the paradox of subjectivation, we remain within the binary conception of agency in terms of subordination and resistance. A consideration of the agency of the pietists requires that we move out of this agonistic and dualistic structure. Finally, the paradox of subjectivation model is problematic because it understands agency as produced only through operations of power. Thus, while it provides an insightful account of relations of power, it cannot account for other kinds of relations. Thus, another model is needed to account for the development of the pietists' agency through love for God and desire for closeness to God.

At this point, it should be noted that in fact it is Butler, not Foucault, who defines agency in terms of the "paradox of subjectivation."[10] Oddly, while her analysis of the women in the mosque movement is framed within Foucault's theory of the ethics of the self, Mahmood never acknowledges that for Foucault the practices of the self-creation that he discusses can be understood as practices of freedom. Later I shall argue that the pietists' agency can be understood within a Foucaultian analysis as a practice of freedom. But I also argue that it is possible to go beyond this analysis to understand the pietists' agency as a practice of freedom as belonging.

Liberal Models of Freedom

Mahmood argues that liberal conceptions of freedom are inadequate to account for the agency of the women in the mosque movement. Her account of liberal freedom focuses on the concepts of negative and positive freedom, where negative freedom refers to the absence of interference, and positive freedom is the capacity to realize an autonomous will. Mahmood notes that the ideal of self-realization precedes the liberal tradition, and can be found in ancient Greek as well as Buddhism and a variety of mystical traditions, including Islam and Christianity; but only in liberalism is the process of realizing oneself understood to be a process of realizing one's own, true will. And she claims that both negative and positive conceptions of freedom rest on the concept of individual autonomy, which follows a procedural principle: "in order for an individual to be free, her actions *must* be the consequence of her 'own will' rather than of custom, tradition or social coercion." Thus, "even illiberal actions can arguably be tolerated if it is determined that they are undertaken by a freely consenting individual who is acting of her own accord" (11). While it can be argued that the women in the mosque movement can be understood as liberal autonomous agents because they are choosing to take up the practices of piety, Mahmood argues that this attempt to account for their agency within a liberal discourse of freedom presupposes that there is "a natural disjuncture between a person's 'true' desires and those that are socially prescribed.... The model of self presupposed by this position dramatically contrasts with the one that conceptually and practically shaped the activities of the women I worked with. The account I have presented of the mosque movement shows that the distinction between the subject's real desires and obligatory social conventions—a distinction at the center of liberal, and at times progressive, thought—cannot be assumed, precisely because socially prescribed forms of behavior constitute the conditions for the emergence of the self as such and are integral to its realization" (149).[11]

While Mahmood argues persuasively that liberal conceptions of freedom that oppose desires to social conventions cannot account for the agency of the pietists, she very often appears to assume that no other conceptions of freedom exist. When she writes, for example, that "freedom is normative to feminism as it is to liberalism" and criticizes the "naturalization of freedom as a social ideal" (10) her focus is not on a particular conception of freedom but on freedom *tout court*. Similarly, when she criticizes the "positing of women's agency as consubstantial with resistance to relations of domination" and questions "the universality of the desire to be free from relations of subordination" (10) she is criticizing feminism's focus not only on liberal proceduralist models of freedom but on any ideal of freedom. No alternative conceptions of freedom are ever discussed. Thus, Mahmood's question as to how we might *reconceive* freedom is asked in a vacuum, as if there were no other conceptions of freedom but the proceduralist conception that she describes.

As I have argued, Mahmood's claim that we can understand the agency of the pietists only if we question the feminist focus on freedom rests on her own assumption that practices of freedom are necessarily practices of resistance to norms. She is implicitly accepting a definition of freedom as negative freedom: freedom from constraints imposed by others, in this case by social norms. Thus, she is unable to develop an account of the pietists' practices as practices of freedom.

In my discussion of positive freedom later in this chapter, I shall argue that liberal conceptions of freedom cannot be reduced to the opposition between desires and social norms, and moreover, that positive freedom cannot be reduced to the procedural account that Mahmood criticizes. I shall argue, further, that the pietists' practices can be understood within several diverse conceptions of freedom.

Freedom as a Practice of Belonging

To address Mahmood's question—"how do we conceive of individual freedom in a context where the distinction between the subject's own desires and socially prescribed performances cannot be easily presumed, and where submission to certain forms of (external) authority is a condition for achieving the subject's potentiality?"—we need to go beyond the liberal conception of freedom that Mahmood criticizes, and also beyond the formulation of agency as an effect of operations of power, and beyond the paradox of subjectivation, to a conception of agency and of freedom as a practice of connection and belonging. This requires the recognition that we are not only subjected through operations of power; we are also subjects of relations of reciprocity, mutuality, love, and care.

The question posed by Mahmood is answered differently by communitarians and relational feminists and theorists of communicative action. All of these theorists argue against the view that individual freedom requires an oppositional or atomistic view of the self; they argue that the self is necessarily embedded in social relationships and social horizons, and that one's own desires are formed only within these relationships and horizons. Thus, they recognize that the distinction between social conventions and individual desires is never entirely clear; that in fact individual desires are always shaped by social conventions. But they do not see this process as necessarily oppressive. These theorists distinguish between processes of subjection through subordination to norms that are prescribed or imposed by a society, and processes of social development through social relations that are relations of care, mutuality and love, and through aspirations to ideals that are shared, and which are not oppressive but enabling.

Rather than assuming that social conventions are necessarily both oppressive and enabling, feminist theorists of relational autonomy argue that it is essential to focus on the embeddedness of subjects in social relations in order "to distinguish between those structures of relationship that foster autonomy and those that undermine it."[12] Thus, for example, "inhabiting norms" or social conventions of equality and freedom is enabling, whereas inhabiting norms of feminine subordination is oppressive. This distinction is important.

But there are two problems that arise from it. First, it misses what the paradox of subjectivation recognizes: that very often it is precisely the norms that subordinate that are also those that enable. In the case of the women in the mosque movement, to the extent that they are inhabiting norms of submission to authority, the paradox of subjectivation provides a better account of their agency. But this account cannot make sense of the pietists' struggles to realize a connection with God that, for them, is not oppressive; this requires an account of the pietists as subjects of desires for connection and belonging that are not reducible to operations of power. Thus, these two paradigms are complementary, and need to be combined in order to produce a more nuanced account of the production of agency.

The second problem is more fundamental: the relational autonomy perspective assumes that social relations and norms can be distinguished in terms of whether they produce autonomy. And the problem is that the women in the mosque movement are not concerned with the development of autonomy. Mahmood argues that liberal communitarians and relational feminists cannot account for the agency of the pietists, because freedom for these thinkers still depends on "the ability to distance oneself from the social" (150). Thus, these thinkers still rely on a liberal model of freedom, according to which autonomy is defined procedurally as the capacity to realize one's own will. Mahmood notes that Charles Taylor argues for a conception of positive freedom characterized by the capacity to achieve "a certain condition of self-clairvoyance and self-understanding in order to be able to prioritize and assess conflicting desires, fears, and aspirations within oneself" (Mahmood,150).[13] Similarly, Seyla Benhabib argues for "a balance between social belonging and critical reflection wherein critical reflection is understood fundamentally as an autonomous exercise" (Mahmood,151).[14] As Mahmood points out, "Ultimately a person for whom self-realization is a matter of "self clairvoyance"—sorting out one's own interests from those that are social and collective—looks to a different set of strategies and horizons than a subject for whom the principal ideals and tools of self-reference reside outside of herself" (151). The pietists are not striving to realize ends that can be located within the self; the ends they want to realize are God's. As I shall argue, for the pietists, belonging or connection to God is itself the goal they are working towards; further, I am suggesting that for the pietists this belonging *is* freedom. To address Mahmood's question, then, we need another formulation of agency and of freedom as a practice of belonging. In the remainder of this paper, I shall develop this alternative paradigm by taking up four conceptions of freedom that emerge from Mahmood's analysis.

Alternative Conceptions of Freedom

1. Freedom as Self-Creation: Freedom as Inhabiting Norms or Inhabiting Connections

In his late work on the ethics of the self, Michel Foucault was working on a conception of agency, and of freedom, as the practice of self-creation. Foucault turned to the ancient Greeks as a model because they exemplified an ethical practice and an understanding of ethics very different from the modern focus on conformity to universal moral laws. For Foucault, the appeal of the Greek ethics was that the focus of ethics was not the relation to a universal (God or a moral code) outside oneself, but the relationship to oneself: the *mode of subjection* to moral precepts was not obedience to an external law but the creation of a beautiful self, and the *telos* of the practice was not some external ideal but self-mastery itself. For Foucault, this alternative form of ethics offers a possibility of *freedom*: freedom through practices of self-creation. For the Greeks, Foucault argues, "nobody is obliged [by moral laws] to behave in such a way as to be truthful to their wives, to not touch boys, and so on. But if they want to have a beautiful existence, if they want to have a good reputation, if they want to be able to rule others, they have to do that. So they accept those obligations in a conscious way for the beauty or glory of existence. The choice, the aesthetic choice or the political choice, for which they decide to accept this kind of existence—that's the *mode d'assujettissement*. It's a choice, it's a personal choice" (Foucault 1984b, 356).

While Foucault invoked Greek ethics as a model for freedom, he argued that all ethical frameworks could be analyzed in terms of four elements of ethical self-relation: the substance of ethics, the mode of subjectivation, the operations, and the telos of the practice. Following Foucault, Mahmood analyzes the agency of the women in the mosque movement in terms of these four elements of ethical self-relation. Mahmood argues that for the pietists, the telos, or ideal, is the exemplary model of the pious self. And the mode of subjectivation is through following the divine law embodied in the Quran and Sunna and the exegetical literature: the four main schools of Islamic law produced by Sunni scholars between the second and ninth centuries A.D.[15] But while the mode of subjectivation is obedience to the will of God, Mahmood argues that the form of morality is not strictly juridical. "There are no centralized authorities that enforce the moral code and penalize infractions. Rather, the mosque movement has a strong individualizing impetus that requires each person to adopt ascetic practices for shaping moral conduct. Each individual must interpret the moral codes, in accordance with traditional guidelines, in order to discover how she, as an individual, may best realize the divine plan for her life" (30–1). As Mahmood notes, the pietists engage in daily practices of cultivation of their bodies, their behaviors, and their desires, toward the ideal of realizing the will of God, and living in closeness to God. Mahmood argues that the movements of the body comprise the primary material substance upon which various techniques of ethical self-relation are practiced, and that ascetic practices on the body are combined with practices that establish coordination between inner states (desires, thoughts) and outer conduct (gestures, actions, speech) (31).

For the pietists, the practice of wearing the veil, for example, is not, as it is for many Muslim women, merely symbolic. As many scholars have noted, the meanings of the veil vary across cultures and contexts: the veil can work as a symbol of religiosity, of piety and modesty, of women's subordination, of feminism, of Islamic identity, and of urban sophistication and education, among other meanings.[16] While some of these meanings are accepted by the pietists, for them, wearing the veil is not primarily a symbolic act but a discipline through which the ideals of piety and modesty before God are enacted. Through wearing the veil, through prayer, and through other daily practices, the women in the mosque movement cultivate their closeness to God.

Clearly, the women in the mosque movement are not engaged in the kinds of practices of freedom that Foucault idealized: they do not act according to personal choice with a view to developing a beautiful self. They are submitting to the will of God in order to develop pious selves. It might be argued that submission to God's will is imposed by no one but themselves: they are choosing to follow this path, and they exercise considerable individual choice and interpretation in determining how best to practice piety. Like the virtuoso pianist, they are engaged in particular disciplines to achieve their desired goal. Mahmood argues, however, that it would be wrong to assimilate this practice into the framework of liberal choice, because the point of the practice is not to follow one's own truth or desire, but to conform to God's. For Mahmood, Foucault's analytical model offers an alternative to the liberal model: it allows us to understand the pietists' agency as a practice of *inhabiting norms*. Though Mahmood does not describe this practice as a practice of freedom, it might be said that the pietists are like the ancient Greeks in that they conform to particular norms not because they are obliged by universally recognized laws to do so, but because they aspire to a particular telos or ideal of self: the pious self. So we can say that the pietists are engaged in practices of self-creation through particular ways of inhabiting norms, and that these are practices of freedom.

Mahmood frames her discussion of these practices within Foucault's analysis of agency in terms of the operations of power through which subjectivation proceeds, and this analysis does show how the pietists' agency is produced through their own ascetic practices on their bodies, and on their souls. I want to argue, however, that Mahmood's description of the practices exceeds this framework, for the pietists' disciplinary practices are not fully analyzable in terms of operations of power directed towards inhabiting norms and toward the achievement of a pious self. The pietists are not focused only on *submission* to God; they are also engaged in the creation of a different kind of *connection* to God. As Mahmood notes, "The women I worked with described the condition of piety as the quality of 'being close to God': a manner of being and acting that suffuses all of one's acts, both religious and worldly in character" (122). But this relationship is submerged in Mahmood's account. For instance, while Mahmood notes that the pietists work to cultivate the "classical triad" of fear, love, and hope, her analysis focuses on the disposition of fear, and the way in which fear of God works toward the realization of a virtuous life. Thus she focuses on the ways in which submission to God works to produce a pious self. But she does note that the pietists' practices are also practices of hope: "anticipation of closeness to God" and of love: "the affection and devotion one feels for God" (140). And she stresses that these dispositions are not simply motivations for pious behavior; these emotions are "integral aspects of pious action itself" (140). While Mahmood's analysis focuses on how these emotions "come to *command authority* in the topography of a particular moral-passional self" (140; my italics), the stress on love for God and the hope for closeness to God indicates that the pietists themselves are concerned not only with submission in the service of an ideal self, but with another relation altogether. They are concerned not only with *inhabiting norms* but with *inhabiting connections*: they are practicing connections to God.

Thus, for the women in the mosque movement, the practice of wearing the veil cannot be understood solely as a practice of "inhabiting norms" through which a subject is produced. While the pietists are certainly inhabiting norms, and while submission to God's will is one mode of these practices, the pietists are engaged in the creation of a connection to God. Their work on themselves is focused not only on the creation of a pious self, but also, and for them more importantly, on this connection with God. The ideal they are striving toward is a state called *khushu:* "being in the presence of God" (123). I am arguing, then, that to make sense of the pietists' agency, the *analytical framework* of relation to self must be supplemented with an analytical framework of other kinds of relations, in this case, relation to God. Within this framework the *telos* is not the creation of a pious self but connection with God; and the *mode of subjection* is not submission to God's will, and not fear of God, but love for God and hope for connection with God. Finally, the pietists can be understood to be not only *inhabiting norms* but *inhabiting connections*. While Mahmood, following Foucault, recognizes that the pietists' agency involves various kinds of relationships, neither understands those relationships as being the telos of the practice, and neither understands practices of freedom within a framework of inhabiting connections.[17]

These understandings of the pietists' practices in terms of inhabiting norms and inhabiting connections can open up conceptions of freedom that are different from the one that is thematized by Foucault, and different from the conception of agency thematized by Mahmood. These different conceptions of freedom emerge in a discussion among some of the women about the need to cultivate the practice of prayer, and the role of this practice in relation to all of one's daily practices. As one woman notes, "If your mind is mostly occupied with things that are not related to God, then you are in a state of *ghafla* (carelessness, negligence)" (124). On the other hand, "when you do things in a day for God and avoid other things because of Him, it means you're thinking about Him, and therefore it becomes easy for you to strive for Him against yourself and your desires" (125). The emphasis here is on the way in which one's relation to God, and doing things for God, inhabits and transforms all of one's day-to-day activities: what you say to people, how you act, how you feel: "these are the things that have an effect on your heart" (125). If you focus on what annoys you or angers you "then you know that you will just gather more sins, but if you are quiet then you are beginning to organize your affairs on account of God and not in accord with your temperament. And then you will realize that your sister will lose the ability to make you angry, and you will become more desirous of God." Thus, through practice one creates a self-in-relation with God, and this relationship will alter the nature of all of your relationships with others, with yourself, and with the world, in all of the practices of your daily life. "You will begin to notice that if you say the morning prayer, it will also make your daily affairs easier, and if you don't pray it will make them hard" (125).

"It will make your daily affairs easier." This can be interpreted in Beauvoir's terms: by following conventions you make life easy, make yourself happy, lull yourself into acquiescence, but you are failing to be free. I want to suggest two alternative views. First, it can be argued that freedom can be found through *inhabiting norms*: by focusing on an ideal or purpose you find freedom in that focus, which provides a structure within which free play is possible, because you are not distracted by petty annoyances, or by having to make constant life decisions. A set of rules, or structure, provides the constraints that enable freedom of interpretation and free play within that structure: the person following the discipline of daily prayers is able to give herself fully to that practice, just as the pianist is able to lose herself in playing, and focus her attention on the practices of playing. And surely this is true of the focus on any goal or ideal: the focus provides a constraint or set of constraints within which freedom may be enabled. The definition of freedom in terms of the security provided by structure is suggested by Hobbes, who argued that just as water is free to flow through a channel, humans are free to act within the constraints provided by sovereign law.[18] And it may be argued that the important distinction here is between norms that are self-given and norms that are external to one's own will or desires. But what I am calling attention to here is an *experience* of freedom that is found in focus on a purpose, inhabiting norms, a set of constraints; this is a substantive definition of freedom, which is different from a procedural definition of freedom as resistance to norms, or following one's own will or desires. What I am thematizing is the phenomenological dimension of participant experience. This particular experience of freedom is the experience of creativity, of play, of being in the present moment.

Secondly, I want to suggest that a substantive kind of freedom is found not only through inhabiting norms but through *inhabiting connections*. The women in the mosque movement are engaged in relations to themselves, to their bodies and actions, and to others, that realize a self-in-connection, and that aspire to an ideal of freedom in connection with the sacred—an ideal that can be found in many religious teachings, including Eastern teaching traditions and many indigenous traditions, as well as monotheistic traditions, including the Islamic mystic tradition. This is different from the personal relation to God as a friend or confidant that is emphasized in Protestant Christianity, and which Mahmood says is not a feature of the pietists' understanding. This is an understanding of freedom as an experience of connection with the source of life, with the sacred, or divine, or spirit, which gives one a center and by extension connects one with all beings, and with all of life. The common idea is that when one is focused on this connection, then one's daily life becomes lighter, and the lightness one feels is freedom. As the example of the pietist acting in relation to God indicates, the experience of connection with God extends to all of one's relationships. Thus this experience of freedom is an experience of freedom in one's various relationships with others, with oneself, and with the world.

Both of these understandings of substantive freedom—freedom in inhabiting prescribed norms and freedom in inhabiting connections—can be found in the Islamic tradition. The term "Islam" means "submission'" or "peace." Muslims are those who surrender to God's law and as a result are at peace with themselves and with God.[19] In the Islamic mystic tradition, Sufism, this peace can be understood as freedom.[20] This can be understood in two ways. First, freedom (*ḥurriyya*) is understood as "freedom from everything except God and the devotion to Him. It is the recognition of the essential relationship between God the master and His human slaves who are completely dependent on Him, "freedom," as Ibn 'Arabī expresses it, "being perfect slavery."[21] Secondly, "True freedom is attainable only by freeing one's heart from worldly worries and anxieties about the things of this world, and so being able to turn to God with one's whole being."[22] While both of these interpretations define freedom as a relationship, in the first interpretation freedom is clearly equated with submission: enslavement to God. In the second, freedom is understood as a sustaining connection. Both interpretations are clearly opposed to a liberal individualist conception. But they do express a conception of freedom. In this conception, the relation of dependence on God allows for an experience of freedom as peace. Freedom, then, is found in faith: in a life whose meaning is clear and unquestioned. And freedom is found in the connection with God.

While the understanding of freedom as a relationship of enslavement to God is distasteful to liberal sensibilities, what is also being expressed here is the idea that one should be subordinate to no one except God. This has been a powerful idea in the Islamic revival. Leila Ahmed notes, for example, that the leading intellectual of the Muslim Brotherhood in the 1960s, Sayyid Qutb, linked Islamic spirituality with economic and political revolution: "The Islamic system, grounded in social justice and binding Muslims to obedience only to God, simultaneously liberated them, Qutb argued, from subservience to any human being. Islam…wrote Qutb,…' frees us from economic and social disparity, realizing a balanced society while sustaining us spiritually'" (Ahmed 2011, 70–1).[23] Thus, this conception of freedom is linked to the understanding of freedom as resistance to domination, to which I shall return in the last section of this chapter.

2. Positive Freedom

For many theorists of individual positive freedom, the practice of freedom is the capacity to discover and adhere to one's own truth or to follow one's own path. Thus one follows the ideal of being true to oneself: the ideal of authenticity (Taylor 1992). This may require that we experience and learn as much as possible about the world and the paths available to us (Mill), that we are able to critically assess and evaluate our conflicting desires and values (Taylor 1985a, Frankfurt 1998), that we develop autonomy competencies (Meyers 2004), and that we are supported in our processes of self-development and self-realization (Nedelsky 1989, Young 2007).

As Mahmood argues, the pietists' practices are not oriented toward discovering and expressing their own desires, or the authenticity or truth of the self. Thus, she argues that the pietists' agency cannot be understood within a liberal model of positive freedom. Unlike liberal subjects for whom the struggle is to discover and follow the truth within oneself, the women in the mosque movement struggle to discover and follow the truth that is given by God. Thus, the struggle, for the pietists, is not to access or discover their own desires; the struggle is to *cultivate* their desires, to enable a practice of closeness and connection to God. The pietists work on themselves not only to produce pious behaviors—to pray regularly, to behave piously toward others—but to develop the *desire* to pray, the *desire* to behave piously. Thus, the "outward behavioral forms were not only expressions of their interiorized religiosity but also a necessary means of acquiring it" (147). Mahmood points out that the mosque participants she encountered "did not regard authorized models of behavior as an external social imposition that constrained the individual. Rather, they viewed socially prescribed forms of conduct as the potentialities, the 'scaffolding,' if you will, through which the self is realized" (148). And they looked to exemplary models of piety not in order to discover the "true I" but as a means "to *transcend* the "I" that is invested in ephemeral pleasures and pursuits" (147–48). According to this understanding, "action does not issue forth from natural feelings but *creates* them" (157). Thus, for example, one wears the veil not because one feels modest, but in order to create the virtue of modesty before God.

Again, Mahmood argues that the pietists exemplify a conception of agency through conforming to and inhabiting norms, and that this contrasts sharply with liberal models of agency and freedom. But the understanding of freedom as being true to one's desires, or to oneself, hardly exhausts conceptions of positive freedom within liberalism. Mahmood's understanding of liberal freedom as predicated on accessing one's own desires largely ignores the Kantian tradition, according to which autonomy is not the capacity to follow one's own desires, but is rather defined by following the categorical imperative, and by aligning one's will with a universal law.[24] The pietists can be seen to be following the Kantian ideal of autonomy: rather than following their desires, they are following the dictates of a higher law to which they rationally assent. Thus, freedom requires not following their own path but recognizing what is right and transforming themselves so that they actively will and follow that path. The choice, for the pietists, is not between following one's desires and following custom or tradition, but between following one's desires and following the higher law.

Here we can distinguish between conceptions of morality and conceptions of the good life: moral autonomy requires following the categorical imperative, whereas authenticity or personal autonomy requires following one's own path. But in practice, these two are intertwined. As many theorists argue, following one's own path requires assessing and ranking one's desires according to the values and ideals that are most important to us (Taylor 1985a, Frankfurt 1988). Moreover, personal autonomy—the capacity to follow my own path or ends—is justified by the appeal to the right of each individual to be treated as an end. How, for example, should we characterize a feminist practice of individual freedom within these terms? As a feminist, my desire to follow my own path is motivated and legitimated through my appeal to moral ideals of equality, justice, and freedom. And thus, like the pietists, I am following and striving to inhabit norms beyond and above myself. Moreover, I cultivate my desires, and my self-understanding, in part through my appeal to these norms. It may be argued that the important distinction here is between norms that are self-given and norms that are external to one's own will or desires. But just as the pietists are following God's will, isn't the feminist following the ideal of freedom or equality that is similarly assumed to be absolute, and that is taken up as one's own? Nevertheless, it is true that these projects are different: while the feminist is appealing to norms outside herself, she is drawing on them to support her attempt to discover and follow her own true will; whereas the pietist is striving to overcome her own desires, in order to follow God, and to cultivate her desires so that they align with God's will.

In any case, Mahmood's argument that positive freedom necessarily rests on a proceduralist account according to which one follows one's own desires or will is in fact wrong. Conceptions of positive freedom are quite wide-ranging: they include, among other things, the capacity to make choices and reflect on alternatives, the capacity to control one's own life, and the capacity to participate in collective self-government. It can be argued that the pietists do all of these things. The women's mosque movement is a movement to democratize the interpretation of Islamic texts and to assert women's individual and collective agency: women themselves are taking collective and individual control of the interpretation of texts and the application of teachings to their own lives.

But even if we focus on an understanding of positive freedom as individual self-realization, it is not the case that this necessarily involves following one's own desires or will. As Charles Taylor argues, positive freedom is distinguished from negative freedom in that it is an "exercise concept" rather than an "opportunity concept": positive freedom is characterized by the achievement of, not just the opportunity for, self realization (Taylor 1985b). Thus, while negative freedom is characterized by the absence of constraint, which allows me to do as I want, positive freedom requires the realization of an ideal. According to this understanding, positive freedom is a substantive, not a proceduralist conception of freedom: we are free only when we realize a particular substantive ideal. Freedom is a state of being. While Taylor argues that what constitutes self-realization is specific to the individual, and thus requires, as Mahmood points out, self-clairvoyance, he argues that freedom is not just about doing what you want, but is rather about achieving your "basic purposes." This means that "the subject himself cannot be the final authority on the question whether he is free; for he cannot be the final authority on the question whether his desires are authentic, whether they do or do not frustrate his purposes" (216). Quentin Skinner takes this further. He points out that what underlies neo-Hegelian theories of positive liberty is "the belief that human nature has an essence, and that we are free if and only if we succeed in realizing that essence in our lives" (Skinner, 242). Thus, he writes, those who accept the Aristotelian argument that man is a political animal will believe, with Arendt, that freedom is found in politics, and in action. "More specifically, you will believe that, as Charles Taylor adds, 'freedom resides at least in part in collective control over the common life', because the exercise of such control is the form of activity in which the essence of our humanity is most fully realized" (242). If positive freedom involves realization of an essence that precedes our action, then freedom will lie not in autonomy and not even necessarily in authenticity, i.e., in the realization of a purpose that is specific to the individual. Freedom will be achieved through conformity to that essence. This understanding of positive freedom as the realization of an essence is of particular relevance to the women in the mosque movement. As Skinner writes: "Suppose, for example, that you accept the Christian view that the essence of our nature is religious, and thus that we attain our highest ends if and only if we consecrate our lives to God. Then you will believe that, in the words of Thomas Cranmer, the service of God 'is perfect freedom'" (Skinner, 242). Thus, we can understand the pietists to be striving toward the realization of a substantive ideal of freedom: according to this conception, a life lived in the service of God would be a life lived in perfect freedom.[25]

3. Communitarian Freedom

Following this understanding of positive freedom as the realization of our essence, those who believe, with Aristotle and Hegel, that the human being is a social being understand freedom not as the capacity to realize one's own desires but as the capacity to realize oneself in relationship with others. Thus, for the early Marx, individual freedom is realized only through nonalienated relationships. This is the understanding of freedom that underlies the position of communitarians and relational feminists, and while many argue that communitarianism needs to be supplemented with a liberal proceduralist conception in order to avoid the dangers of totalitarianism and of historical regression to premodern (and preliberal) social orders, others, along with theorists of "alternative modernities," argue that nonliberal communitarian conceptions, common to many indigenous, African, and Asian traditional worldviews (in other words, the worldviews of most of the world's peoples), provide an understanding of relational being that is more likely to sustain human beings and the earth.

   As Mahmood notes, since the 1970s, in response to white middle-class feminists' critique of the nuclear family, Indigenous and Black feminists have argued that freedom, for them, consists in being able to restore and sustain families and communities, which have been broken by long histories of slavery, genocide, and racism (13). Oddly, Mahmood takes these arguments as simply expanding the concepts of negative and positive freedom, "forcing feminists to rethink the concept of individual autonomy in light of other issues" (13). But these arguments point to a more radical critique of liberal autonomy, and to another form of freedom. In chapter 2 I discussed the kind of freedom invoked by Frederick Douglass, and in the alternative modernism of the "love and justice tradition of Black America," by Toni Morrison and Patricia Hill Collins and Cynthia Willett. In this tradition, in which "freedom lives or dies in the relationships forged between persons," freedom is located in home and understood as a social and ethical force: "spirit." There I argued that this understanding of freedom goes beyond situating freedom in the context of relationships: instead, freedom is the capacity to be in relationships one desires, and to expand oneself through relationship. A consideration of the women in the mosque movement takes this further: freedom is located in the sustaining of a particular relationship; in this case the relationship with God. It might even be suggested that for the pietists, freedom is the capacity to desire a relationship that is not necessarily chosen. In particular, freedom is found in the cultivation of desire for connection with God. But this is not just an extension but an inversion of the idea that freedom is the capacity to be in relationships one desires.[26]

The danger of such a conception of freedom—freedom to be in and to desire relationships that are not necessarily chosen—is that it can leave us open to quietism, to acceptance of domination and abuse. And that is why feminist theorists of relational autonomy, while they stress the embeddedness of agents in relationships, also stress the importance of distinguishing between supportive and oppressive relationships. As Iris Young notes, relational autonomy "entails recognizing that agents are related in many ways that they have not chosen." But it also entails recognizing that in these relationships "agents are able either to thwart one another or support one another. Relational autonomy consists partly, then, in the structuring of relationships so that they support the maximal pursuit of individual ends" (Young, 47). Thus, for Young, the pursuit of individual ends remains paramount.

But relational feminist and care ethics arguments also point to a different conception of freedom. As many feminist theorists have pointed out, the model of the self as free chooser grossly misrepresents the reality of individual agency. In "Non-Contractual Society" Virginia Held argued that political philosophy would be very different if we began not from the perspective of atomistic individuals who choose to relate to others through contracts, in order to avoid others' unwarranted interventions, but from the perspective of mothers who are already in relations with dependent others (Held, 1987). It would surely be wrong to argue that freedom for the mother requires that the relation with her child must support the maximal pursuit of her own ends. If we take this relationship as paradigmatic, then perhaps one kind of freedom is not so much the capacity to choose your own ends, and is not just the capacity to love whom you choose to love, but is the capacity to sustain a relationship: the capacity to love and care for your child. And we can then distinguish between relationships that support or thwart that relationship as an end: freedom then might require a society that supports your capacity to care for your child.[27] Does such an argument confuse freedom with a good life or with justice? Or does it problematize a purely individualistic and self-centered conception of freedom and point to another conception of freedom?

Many Indigenous and African American women have argued that freedom for them is the capacity to rebuild and sustain their communities, even if these communities may not maximize their individual ends. Some Indigenous women have argued that their identities as traditional landowners, their links to and responsibilities for their country, and their roles as cultural custodians who can pass on cultural traditions to their children precede claims for individual rights and are central to their freedom.[28] Freedom, then, is understood in terms of connection to land and to community. According to this conception, the connection to land and community *is* the end, not because I choose it but because its claim is greater than my choices. Similarly, for the mosque women, God's claim is greater than mine. And the path to freedom is to create an authentic connection with that source. We might learn from the women in the mosque movement and from Indigenous women that the question as to whether our connections are chosen or not is not always the most important question in a practice of freedom. Freedom can involve accepting our connections (to land, to God, to children, to community) and learning to practice our connections differently. (To draw an analogy: one does not choose one's body. Is transformation of that body to fit with an ideal the best path to freedom? Or is freedom found in transforming one's connection to the body one has?)

This understanding of freedom in connection is a substantive freedom that is very different from the procedural understanding of freedom as following one's own desires. It is also different from an understanding of collective group freedom that is predicated on positive freedom, with the group simply taking the place of the individual. Yet the particular end of freedom in connection is one that most can recognize: freedom as the pursuit of a place where one can be at home. As Charles Taylor notes, the ideal of authenticity, or following one's own truth, has its roots in earlier ethical views, where "being in touch with some source—for example God, or the Idea of the Good—was considered essential to full being" (Taylor 1992, 28). So it can be argued that the idea of "being in touch with some source" is what liberal and other conceptions of freedom hold in common.

The question left unanswered by a conception of freedom as accepting and sustaining our connections is: how can we know when accepting our connections is an enactment of freedom and when it is a capitulation to domination? But this question can be asked of a conception of freedom based in autonomy as well: how do I know whether the path I choose is a path of freedom? The question is resolved in the proceduralist model: my choosing or willing it is what defines it as free. This leaves the question of substantive ends entirely open. But that is the question that liberal models cannot answer. How do I know whether the path—or the relationships—I choose will serve a substantive end of freedom?[29] For the pietists, the substantive end is given by God, and that is a more reliable place to start than my own will. I do think that the idea that freedom can be located in sustaining a relationship that one has not chosen is difficult to uphold unless one in fact endorses that relationship as an end. The pietists certainly do endorse the relationship with God as an end. (And they do also reflect on alternative possibilities.) And so they can be said to choose it. The difference, for the pietists, is that the choice does not originate with themselves.

None of this, of course, addresses the objection that a conception of freedom that does not prioritize individual rights leaves individuals open to oppression. Many Islamic feminists, along with many Indigenous and African American feminists, argue that women's individual rights must not be trumped by obligations to God or to land or community. And many are finding new ways of integrating these different interests.[30] In the following section, I shall discuss the ways that the women in the mosque movement are able to resist oppression from within this alternative conception of freedom.

4. Critique and Resistance

Capacities for questioning, critique, and resistance are central to modern conceptions of freedom. As James Tully notes, "Modern constitutionalism enthrones the freedom of critical enquiry and dissent by excluding the authority of custom" (Tully 1995, 202). While Foucault's understanding of freedom is drawn in part from the ideal of self-creation that he found in the ancient Greeks, Foucault also argued very strongly for a conception of freedom as resistance: in "What is Enlightenment," he argues for a conception of modern freedom as critique, as resistance to what is (Foucault, 1984a).[31] Philip Pettit and Iris Young argue for conceptions of freedom as non domination (Pettit 1997, Young 2007). Nancy Hirschmann argues that a feminist theory of freedom must involve a critique of patriarchal oppression and male dominance (Hirschmann 2003).[32]

There are in fact many ways in which critique and resistance do play a central role in the practices of the pietists. Their very presence in the mosques, where they gather to study under female teachers, constitutes a resistance to the tradition of male dominance and to the mosques as men's domain. Women engage in the piety movement often against the protests of their more secular husbands, and use various strategies to persuade their husbands and other male relatives to become more pious themselves. Moreover, the piety movement, as part of the Islamic revival, is based on a critique of the encroaching secularism of daily life in Egypt, and, by extension, of western imperialism. It should also be noted that the pietists very definitely do not passively accept the teachings of the Imams; instruction is given by women scholars who are interpreting multiple juridical texts, and the students engage in questioning and argument, so that in the end each woman's interpretation is her own. In all of these practices, the pietists use the discourse of rights and of freedom of choice. So questioning, critique, and resistance are very definitely elements of the pietists' agency.

Yet Mahmood argues that the pietists exemplify a mode of agency that is not predicated on resistance. Instead, she presents a complex account of the pietists' practices to show that questioning and critique are subsumed within and integral to a practice of inhabiting norms of piety. It is important to recognize that the pietists are not simply conforming to dominant cultural norms. There are many competing cultures and discourses in Egypt: liberal secularism and feminism have played important roles in Egyptian culture through the past century, and Egypt has a very long history of religious pluralism. The pietists are also not simply conforming to the ideals and politics of the Islamic revival as defined by the Muslim Brotherhood, whose leaders regard the pietists as insufficiently political. Moreover, Islamic doctrine is interpreted very differently by disparate individuals and groups. Mahmood shows that the pietists' agency incorporates competing discourses—so their acts of questioning and critique, and their appeal to rights and choices, are influenced by both liberalism and feminism, as well as nationalism and the Islamic revival movement. As Mahmood notes, in Egyptian culture the histories of Islamism and secular liberalism, as well as nationalism and feminism, are intimately connected, "a connection that is, nonetheless, saturated with tensions and ambivalences" (70).

Given the complexity of these competing discourses and the ways they are taken up, the framing of agency as the capacity to resist conventions is problematic: which conventions, and which norms, should be resisted? On what grounds? We might answer that all should be open to question and critique, and that the process of critique requires making judgments to make distinctions among conventions, such that only those that are oppressive should be resisted. But this begs a further question: oppressive of what? These questions are raised in the case of a woman who uses various tactics to induce her husband to take up more pious behaviors, and to accept her own. The woman, Abir, had joined the mosque movement after a secular upbringing, and her husband resisted her "backwardness," making it clear that he wanted a "more worldly and stylish" wife (176). Abir states resolutely that she will never submit to his authority and give up her practice, "No! Even if he took an absolute stand on the issue...I would not give up da'wa" (177). Mahmood notes that Abir is able to take this position in part because "she could claim a higher moral ground than her husband. Her training in da'wa had given her substantial authority from which to speak and challenge her husband on issues of proper Islamic conduct" (179). Thus, Mahmood argues: "Paradoxically,

Abir's ability to break from the norms of what it meant to be a dutiful wife were predicated upon her learning to perfect a tradition that accorded her a subordinate status to her husband. Abir's divergence from approved standards of wifely conduct, therefore, did not represent a break with the significatory system of Islamic norms, but was saturated with them, and enabled by the capacities that the practice of these norms endowed her with" (179). Mahmood notes that Abir's actions are not motivated by the desire to resist her husband's authority, which in principle she does not contest, but by the desire to correct his impious behavior, and to uphold her own obligations toward God. Thus, she argues that "Abir's complicated evaluations and decisions were aimed toward goals whose sense is not captured by terms such as *obedience* versus *resistance*, or *submission* versus *rebellion*. . . . Abir's defiance of social and patriarchal norms is, therefore, best explored through an analysis of the *ends* toward which it was aimed" (180).

Mahmood's argument rests on her observation that Abir breaks from the norm of subordination to her husband only by upholding and inhabiting other norms: the norms of the practice of Muslim piety. Yet surely the term "resistance" does in fact express Abir's actions. Mahmood seems to be suggesting that the term "resistance" is appropriate only when one resists any convention or authority, on principle. To be clear, Abir is not resisting convention for its own sake, nor is she resisting authority in order to uphold her own ends. She is resisting her husband's authority because she is committed to a particular end: the end of the realization of piety, and of the fulfillment of her obligations toward God. Thus, she is exercising critical judgment to evaluate norms and to judge which take precedence. The end she is upholding is not her own but God's, and she is resisting whatever thwarts that end. But this is resistance, and it is resistance to domination. For Abir, domination or oppression is understood not as the thwarting of her own ends, but as the thwarting of God's ends. This is not to say that the pietists are not at all self-interested or that they do not resist actions that thwart their own ends, but that as participants in the mosque movement their resistance is focused toward the end of realizing God's will.

Here, I want to argue that these practices of critique and resistance can be understood not simply as acts of resistance to norms, and not simply as ways of inhabiting other norms; they can also be understood as practices of *reworking and renegotiating connections,* and thereby renegotiating and transforming their identities. The pietists are working on their connections to the mosques, to their husbands, to each other, to Islam, to secularism, and to themselves, as well as to God, and are thereby transforming their identities as Muslim women. For example, their resistance to their husbands is understandable not in terms of simple opposition but as a renegotiation of their relationships: through strategies of resistance, they in fact establish more equitable relationships. The process of renegotiating connections can be understood as a process of engaging in strategic relations of power, with the aim of changing the balance of power; I would argue that for the pietists it is understood as a process of working within relationships, toward an ideal of being in relations that support and sustain their relation to God.

Finally, it is impossible to understand the women in the mosque movement without recognizing that they are participants in the resistance movement that is the Islamic revival. While Mahmood notes that the piety movement "is only marginally organized around questions of rights, recognition, and political representation" (193) and while the pietists are critical of those Muslims who understand their religious practices primarily as an expression of the Muslim or Arab political identity (and political leaders in turn criticize the mosque participants for pursuing a form of religiosity that is devoid of any sociopolitical effects), Mahmood argues that it would be wrong to conclude that the piety movement has no direct political implications. She quotes Charles Hirschkind's argument that "to the extent that the institutions enabling the cultivation of religious virtue have become subsumed within (and transformed by) the legal and administrative structures linked to the state, then the (traditional) project of preserving those virtues will necessarily be political if it is to succeed" (Mahmood, 193).[33] Hence, Mahmood writes, "It is not surprising therefore, that the supposedly apolitical practices of the piety movement have been continually targeted by the disciplinary mechanisms of the Egyptian state" (194).

I would argue that it is possible to understand the piety movement as a solidarity movement, part of a tradition of freedom as resistance to colonial oppression. This tradition is identified briefly by Isaiah Berlin as a third form of freedom, after negative and positive freedom: "social freedom."[34] Cynthia Willett argues that social freedom, the freedom of solidarity, deconstructs the liberal dualism between autonomy and dependency, bringing us back to a conception of freedom of belonging, and a recognition of interdependence, in the freedom of belonging to cooperative communities (Willett 2008).

Despite her recognition of the political relevance of the women's mosque movement, Mahmood argues that this movement should not be understood as a Islamist political movement, and is not an identity movement. She notes that the pietists themselves distinguish between customary and religious acts, and are critical of Islamist political organizations that regard practices such as veiling as mere symbols of Islamic identity and culture. Mahmood writes that while the pietists do not entirely disagree with the belief that the veil is a symbol of identity and culture, their focus is on making the society more religiously devout. Thus, she writes, the mosque movement is aimed "not toward *recognition* but rather toward the *retraining* of ethical sensibilities so as to create a new social and moral order" (193). But Mahmood's claim that the mosque movement is not an identity movement is based on a very superficial understanding of identity. She writes that the pietists are critical of the understanding of Islamic practices as "little more than markers of identity" (51). But such an analysis equates identity with mere labeling, and with custom. In fact, the project of bringing religious practice back into public life is a central focus of the political movement of the Islamic revival, not only because religious practice is seen as a symbol, but because what has been lost with colonization and globalization is Islamic religious practices a focus of people's lives and an essential source of their connection with their of communities and with their God. As Mahmood herself notes, the political resistance of the Muslim Brotherhood incorporates as a central focus bringing religious practice back into public life. Thus, the project of sustaining Muslim identity and the project of bringing religious practice into everyday life are deeply conjoined. As Leila Ahmed shows in her study of the resurgence of the veil, the Islamic revival in Egypt has been a movement for social justice grounded in the understanding that Islamic faith is a source of liberation. From the beginning, this has been a movement promoting a just social and economic order grounded in Islamic principles (Ahmed 2011).[35] Mahmood's claim that the women's mosque movement is not an identity movement because it is aimed "not toward *recognition* but rather toward the *retraining* of ethical sensibilities so as to create a new social and moral order" (193) is based on the assumption that an identity movement can aim only toward recognition. I would argue that insofar as they are focused on the retraining of ethical sensibilities so as to create a new Islamic social and moral order, and insofar as they are claiming the right of women to participate in the creation of that order, the women in the mosque movement are engaged in the transformations of their identities, and in attempts to transform Islamic identity.

Toward a Feminist Reconception of Freedom

Finally, I would like to suggest that while the women's mosque movement does not claim to be a feminist movement, the analysis of this movement might lead toward a feminist reconceptualization of freedom through connection, or belonging. Certainly the Islamic revival is a pointed rebuke against the atomism and possessive individualism of western culture. It is also a rebuke against the freedom of choice that empowers women with, as a Muslim woman who spoke at a recent rally in my city put it, "the freedom to undress for men." These challenges to the emptiness of western ideals in which we stylize ourselves as independent and free choosers *can* be taken as critiques of freedom itself and of western ideals altogether; they can also be taken as a challenge to particular conceptions of freedom, a challenge that can provoke us—westerners as well as, perhaps, the women in this movement—to rethink what freedom might mean. And, in particular, to rethink the relationship between freedom and belonging.

The piety movement suggests that freedom can be found in belonging to a defining community, in which one feels supported to explore and to strengthen one's relationships to one's ideals—to acknowledge that one is never the author or origin of the ideal but can only try to connect with it through practices of belonging.

Certainly Western feminist theorists have long been engaged in critiques of the ideal of unencumbered independence, and with the feminist revolution of the past couple of decades, western women are discovering first-hand that the ideal of freedom as nonintervention or independence is unrealizable, so long as we have children and families and/or lives outside of work. Unrealizable, and in fact undesirable. What we need, perhaps, is an ideal of freedom as the condition of being supported in our care for each other, a freedom that is the capacity to participate fully in our relationships with each other, with whom and with what we love.

Notes

1. Abu-Lughod 2002. There is a huge literature on feminism, the veil, and women in Islam. Feminist discussions of the veil and of women in Islam include Ahmed 1992, 2011, Bullock 2002, Lazreg 2009, Mernissi 1992, 2001, Nouraie-Simone 2005, Razack 2008, Scott 2007, Wadud 2006, Hirschmann 2003, Moghadam 1994.
2. See, for example, Alcoff 2006, Cohen et al. 1999, Phillips 2009, Schachar 2001.
3. Narayan 1997, 2000.
4. See, for example, Narayan 2000, Ferguson 2000.
5. See Gibson-Graham 2006.
6. See Brown 1995.
7. It can be argued, of course, that it is very often the case that when western women are in leadership positions in the public sphere, they experience pressure to

compensate by displaying the feminine virtues appropriate to a good wife, mother, and homemaker, as well as signs of subordinate femininity. See Bartky 1990.

8. The same sentence is repeated on p. 149.

9. To be clear: Foucault understands power as productive, not oppressive. But in arguing that agency is "a capacity for action that specific relations of *subordination* create and enable" (18) Mahmood, with Foucault, is arguing that operations of power are operations of subordination, and that these operations produce relations of oppression or domination. For an incisive discussion of the distinction and indistinction between the concepts of power and domination in Foucault's work, see "The Impurity of Practical Reason: Power and Autonomy in Foucault," in Allen 2008. For critiques of Foucault's narrow conception of social relations as only strategic relations, and the argument that this excludes relations based on communication, reciprocity, and mutual recognition, see Allen 2008, 68–71, and McNay 1992, 163–165. Allen argues that while Foucault does not theorize nonstrategic relations he also does not foreclose the possibility of such relations.

10. Butler uses this phrase extensively in *The Psychic Life of Power*. I discuss Butler's understanding of the paradox in the Introduction to this book.

11. Mahmood's argument that liberal conceptions of freedom presuppose "a natural disjuncture between a person's 'true' desires and those that are socially prescribed" contains a number of contestable claims. Later in this chapter I argue that liberalism does not necessarily rest on the actualization of desires. I do not agree that liberalism necessarily assumes that this disjuncture is "natural," but I do not have the space to discuss this claim here.

12. Nedelsky 2011, 122–123.

13. Quoting Taylor 1985, 229.

14. Referring to Benhabib 1992.

15. See Mahmood, 46, 57, 81.

16. See Abu-Lughod 2002, Ahmed 1992, 2011, Lazreg 2009, Mernissi 1992, Wadud 1999, 2006.

17. In a later essay, Mahmood does focus on the nature of the connection between the pious self and the Prophet Muhammed. She draws on Aristotle's conception of *schesis*, understood as an embodied habitation and intimate proximity that imbues a particular modality of relation, to describe this relationship as "the result of a labor of love in which one is bound to the authorial figure through a sense of intimacy and desire. It is not due to the compulsion of 'the law' that one emulates the Prophet's conduct, therefore, but because of the ethical capacities one has developed that incline one to behave in a certain way" (Mahmood 2009, 78).

18. Hobbes, Thomas. 1982. *Leviathan*. Ed. C.B. Macpherson. New York: Viking.

19. "The term *islām* is derived from the Arabic root *s-l-m*, which means submission or peace. Muslims are those who surrender to God's will or law and as a result,

Muslims believe, are at peace with themselves and with God. To embrace Islam is to become a member of a worldwide faith community (*ummah*). Thus, believers have both an individual and corporate religious identity and responsibility or duty to obey and implement God's will in personal and social life." ("Islam, an Overview," *Oxford Encyclopaedia of the Modern Islamic World*, Oxford Islamic Studies Online)

20. While the pietists follow the Sunni focus on practical disciplines rather than the Sufi focus on inner life, their understanding of Islam comes from a variety of sources, both oral and written. Written sources include the *fiqh*, or interpretation, found in *fiqh* manuals written for the general public, and these also draw on many sources.

21. "Hurriya," *Brill Online Encyclopaedia of Islam*, Second Edition. A similar definition is found in the Oxford Dictionary of Islam: "Hurr: Free. Also hurriyyah, freedom. Hurr and hurriyyah became important metaphysical concepts in Sufism, connoting freedom from everything other than God and devotion to Him. Since humans are the slaves of God, freedom, as Ibn al-Arabi put it, is the perfect form of slavery." (Oxford Dictionary of Islam, Islamic Studies Online)

22. Fethullah Gülen. 2007. *Key Concepts in the Practice of Sufism*. Volume 2. The Fountain Press (accessed online).

23. Qutb was executed by the Nasser government in 1966, and his arguments for the legitimacy of violence were repudiated by the subsequent leadership of the Brotherhood. His ideas regarding liberation remained powerful.

24. Indeed, Foucault's critique of modern liberalism is that it is a code morality, oriented *not* toward following one's own desires but toward subordinating those desires to moral laws. (As I have noted in chapter 1, Foucault also criticizes the imperative to discover the truth of oneself, or one's true desires.)

25. In his classic defense of negative freedom, Isaiah Berlin argues that the fact that conceptions of positive freedom within the liberal tradition allow for such divergent possibilities is a very good reason for rejecting positive freedom. (Berlin 2008).

26. Thanks to Amy Allen for clarifying this point.

27. I develop this argument in "The Global Universal Caregiver."

28. See, for example, Cole et al. 1998. For discussions of this issue see, for example, Blaser et al. 2010, Eisenberg and Jeff Spinner-Halev 2005.

29. As both Marilyn Friedman and Nancy Hirschmann point out, conceptions of positive freedom are unable to resolve the problem of "second guessing": how do we know what our true, or highest, desires really are? See Friedman 2002 and Hirschmann 2003.

30. For Islamic feminism, see Wadud 1999, 2006, Mernisi 1992, and the websites Musawah and Sisters in Islam. There are very active Islamic feminist organizations in Iran and Indonesia.

31. Interestingly, Mahmood never thematizes Foucault's emphasis on resistance.

32. Hirschmann defines freedom as the individual's capacity to make choices and act upon them, and argues that this entails the capacity to reflect on alternatives, to reflect on the context and social construction of choices, and to participate in constructing the conditions of choice. Hirschmann closely analyzes the conditions of women's choices in particular contexts: see in particular her chapter on veiling.

33. Hirschkind 1997, 13.

34. See the discussion of Berlin's third form of freedom in Skinner, 2002.

35. It is surely not necessary to point out that it is also a movement that has often promoted violence, bigotry, and hatred.

IDENTITIES AND FREEDOMS

Through this book I have argued that while identities can be prisons, they can also be sources of freedom. Identities can be bound up with relations of power, and freedom therefore involves critique of our identities. On the other hand, our identities can also bind us together, with sustaining and affirming connections that serve as deep sources of meaning and solidarity, and of freedom. I have argued that identifications with ideals, with others, with collective "we"s and with ourselves can be sources of freedom, but that we need to recognize that these identifications, and hence the freedoms associated with them, open up and require us to confront conflict, difficulty, and complexity: these are the risks of connection.

Still, the question that arises is, how can we know when identities are sources of oppression and when they are sources of freedom? This question is confronted most explicitly in chapter 5: how can we tell when accepting our connections is an enactment of freedom and when it is a capitulation to domination? I have assumed that there is no simple answer to that question. Just as the fact that we are socially constituted makes it impossible to provide a definitive test to determine whether we are acting autonomously—for our deepest desires and commitments are socially shaped, constituted at least in part through internalized norms and values—there is no principle that can determine when identities are sources of oppression and when they are sources of freedom. This problem arises also in the case of negative freedom: given that we are socially shaped, to what extent can I be free from the interference of others? And if the limit of my freedom is action that interferes with the freedom of others, where do we draw that line? Assuming that such questions can be answered only in context, I have worked through issues and cases to untangle the threads of identity that enable our freedom from the threads of identity that imprison, trying to sustain a dialectic between critique and acceptance, transformation and continuity. In chapter 1, I argue that critique of our identities must be an ongoing and open-ended process, since we can never arrive at some absolute truth of the matter, but that we do need to ask questions oriented to truths: to what extent are our identities sources of privilege and effects of oppression? I argue, further, that this question cannot be answered from either a first-person, participant perspective, or a third-person, observer perspective, but must involve a dialectic among perspectives that inform each other. I develop this argument through chapter 5, where I attempt to work through an interaction between the perspectives of liberal and critical feminists, for whom freedom axiomatically involves resistance to subordination, and the women in the mosque movement, who might find freedom through submission to God.

While I stress the importance of critique, chapter 5 explores the limit of a conception of freedom that necessarily includes critique of our identities: here the question is raised as to whether critique of one's identity is in fact necessary for some kinds of freedom. I stress that the women in the mosque movement *do* engage in critique, and that multiple forms of critique—including critiques of western imperialism, of the decline of practices of piety in daily life, of male authority, and of the assumption that women should accept men's interpretations of religious texts—inform their practices. And yet I want to acknowledge that they may have a conception of freedom that does not prioritize critique. This opens another question: whether we should be talking about *freedoms*, in the plural, rather than freedom. Throughout this book, I thematize and argue for a number of different conceptions of freedom, in relation to identities. In chapter 1, I argue for the importance of freedom from fixed identities, and for freedom in practices of resistance that are enabled through practices of identification. But I argue also for a conception of freedom as a meaningful life in connection with others: social freedom. These themes are carried through chapter 2, where I also introduce the conception of freedom as capacity to be in relationships that one desires: to love whom and what you choose to love. This opens up a different conception of relational autonomy and an understanding of freedom in relation to home as the site of a risk of connection. In chapter 3 I focus on freedom through solidarity, arguing that feminist solidarity demands transformations of our identities, and argue for transformative identifications with ideals, with each other, and with particular "we"s as practices of freedom. In chapter 4 I develop the idea of practices of identification as practices of freedom, and continue a discussion of freedom as opening up to otherness and the creation of new connections, new homes. In chapter 5 I argue for a conception of freedom in connections, and trace this through theories of freedom as self-creation, positive freedom, communitarian freedom, and freedom as critique and resistance. All of these are theories of freedom through individual and collective participation in the process of identity construction. Yet they also represent diverse and not always compatible conceptions of freedom.

In *A Secular Age,* Charles Taylor describes an experience that he calls "fullness."

> Somewhere, in some activity, or condition, lies a fullness, a richness; that is, in that place (activity or condition), life is fuller, richer, deeper, more worth while, more admirable, more what it should be. This is perhaps a place of power: we often experience this as deeply moving, as inspiring. Perhaps this sense of fullness is something we just catch glimpses of from afar off…e.g., of peace or wholeness; or…of integrity or generosity or abandonment or self-forgetfulness. But sometimes there will be moments of experienced fullness, of joy and fulfillment, where we feel ourselves there. (Taylor 2007, 5)

Taylor writes that this can be an experience of transcendence of the ordinary, or it may be simply an experience of what has been called "flow," which is found in "moments when the deep divisions, distractions, worries, sadnesses that seem to drag us down are somehow dissolved, or brought into alignment, so that we feel united, moving forward, suddenly capable and full of energy" (6). As Taylor notes, this is the experience that Schiller called "play." As Minnie Bruce Pratt writes, this can look like a childish place; but it can also be seen as " not a childish place.…a place of mutuality, companionship, creativity, sensuousness, easiness in the body, curiosity…hope…safety and love" (Pratt, 24). Taylor identifies this experience with spirituality. But it is also one conception of freedom. As I have noted in chapter 5, it is this conception of freedom that we find in many eastern philosophies and in many religious teachings. It can be understood as a capacity to lose the self, or a capacity for a different experience of self as connected to a universal. And it can be seen as one kind of positive freedom, insofar as it is a substantive state of being that is desired, or that is true or essential. But what are we to make of the fact that this conception of freedom appears to be diametrically opposed to the most popular western conceptions of freedom as absence of interference and as autonomy? On one side we have loss of self and on the other, self-interest and individual will as definitive of freedom. On one side freedom to choose and on the other, freedom from the tyranny of choice. Are we still willing to argue, as Hegel did, that one represents an earlier stage, and the other a more advanced stage of human historical progression? I do not want to give up the moment of negative freedom but I also want to open up the field of what we can recognize as freedoms. This is the risk entailed in acknowledging the existence of multiple alternative modernities.

In his classic essay, "Two Concepts of Liberty," Isaiah Berlin wrote that there exist "more than two hundred" definitions of freedom (Berlin 2008, 168). He proceeded to argue that negative freedom is the only form of freedom worthy of the name, and that the others are category confusions that lead straight to totalitarian regimes—but at least, unlike most contemporary western political philosophers, he did acknowledge their existence.

One of the ideas I develop through this book is a conception of freedom as the condition of being in relations that one can critically affirm. James Tully distinguishes between struggles *of* and struggles *for* freedom (Tully 2008). Drawing on this distinction, I want to distinguish between practices of freedom, which include practices of connection and identification, and an ideal towards which these practices are oriented: a condition of being in relations that we can critically affirm. Thus, one aim of our practices of freedom can be the creation of better relations; for example, relations of equal recognition as opposed to relations of domination.

But while I argue for an understanding of freedom in relationship, I also want to open up the possibility of a plurality of conceptions of freedom. While I have been finishing this book, popular uprisings and revolutions have swept across the Middle East and North Africa, and the Occupy movement has spread to hundreds of cities and towns around the world. While these are all struggles for freedom, and while they share a resistance to domination and to social injustice, they do not all emerge from the same convictions, nor do they all aim toward the same kind of freedom. If Foucault was right to suggest that what defines modernity is the practice of freedom, we need to recognize a plurality of ways of being modern, and a plurality of experiments in freedom. If we are going to recognize a diversity of identities and a diversity of ends in the world, perhaps we need to recognize a diversity of conceptions and practices of freedom, and a diversity of ways of being free.

REFERENCES

Abu-Lughod, Lila. 2002. "Do Muslim Women Really Need Saving?" *American Anthropologist* 104 (3): 783–90.

Ahmed, Leila. 1992. *Women and Gender in Islam: Historical Roots of a Modern Debate*. New Haven: Yale University Press.

Ahmed, Leila. 2011. *A Quiet Revolution: The Veil's Resurgence, From the Middle East to America*. New Haven: Yale University Press.

Ahmed, Sara. 2006. *Queer Phenomenology: Orientations, Objects, Others*. Durham and London: Duke University Press.

Alarcón, Norma. 1990. "The Theoretical Subject(s) of *This Bridge Called My Back* and Anglo-American Feminism." In Gloria Anzaldúa, ed. *Making Face, Making Soul/ Haciendo Caras: Creative and Critical Perspectives by Feminists of Color*. San Francisco: Aunt Lute.

Alcoff, Linda Martín. 1988. Cultural feminism vs. poststructuralism: The identity crisis in feminist theory. *Signs: Journal of Women in Culture and Society* 13 (3): 405–36.

Alcoff, Linda Martín. 2006. *Visible identities: Race, Gender and the Self*. New York: Oxford University Press.

Alcoff, Linda Martín, Michael Hames-Garcia, Satya P. Mohanty, and Paula M. L. Moya. 2006. *Identity Politics Reconsidered*. New York: Palgrave Macmillan.

Allen, Amy. 1999. *The Power of Feminist Theory: Domination, Resistance, Solidarity*. Boulder: Westview Press.

Allen, Amy. 2004. "Foucault, Feminism, and the Self: The Politics of Personal Transformation." In Dianna Taylor and Karen Vintges, ed. *Feminism and the Final Foucault*. Urbana and Chicago: University of Illinois Press, 235–57.

Allen, Amy. 2008. *The Politics of Our Selves: Power, Autonomy, and Gender in Contemporary Critical Theory*. New York: Columbia University Press.

Allen, Anita. 1988. *Uneasy Access*. Totowa, N.J.: Rowman & Littlefield.

Andrews, William. 1987. *Introduction to My Bondage and My Freedom*, by Frederick Douglass. Urbana: University of Illinois Press, xi–xxviii.

Anzaldúa, Gloria. 1987. *Borderlands/La frontera*. San Francisco: Spinsters/Aunt Lute.

Anzaldúa, Gloria, ed. 1990. *Making Face, Making Soul/Haciendo Caras: Creative and Critical Perspectives by Feminists of Color*. San Francisco: Aunt Lute.

Atkinson, Ti-Grace. 1974. *Amazon Odyssey*. New York: Links Books.

Baier, Annette. 1997. *The Commons of the Mind*. Chicago: Open Court.

Balbus, Isaac. 1987. "Disciplining Women: Michel Foucault and the Power of Feminist Discourse." In Seyla Benhabib and Drucilla Cornell, ed. *Feminism as Critique*. Minneapolis: University of Minnesota Press, 110–127.

Bartky, Sandra. 1990. "Foucault, Femininity, and the Modernization of Patriarchal Power." *Femininity and Domination: Studies in the Phenomenology of Oppression*. New York: Routledge.

Beauvoir, Simone de. 1952. *The Second Sex*. Trans. H. M. Parshley . New York: Knopf.

Beauvoir, Simone de. 2010. *The Second Sex*. Trans. Constance Borde and Sheila Malovany-Chevallier. London: Vintage.

Benhabib, Seyla. 1992. *Situating the Self: Gender, Community and Postmodernism in Contemporary Ethics*. New York: Routledge.

Benhabib, Seyla. 1999. "Sexual Difference and Collective Identities: The New Global Constellation." *Signs: Journal of Women in Culture and Society* 24 (2): 335–61.

Benhabib, Seyla. 2002. *The Claims of Culture: Equality and Diversity in the Global Era*. Princeton: Princeton University Press.

Berlin, Isaiah. 2008. "Two Concepts of Liberty." In *Liberty*. Ed. Henry Hardy. Oxford: Oxford University Press, 166–217.

Blaser, Mario, Ravi de Costa, Deborah McGregor, and William D. Coleman, ed. 2010. *Indigenous Peoples and Autonomy: Insights for a Global Age*. Vancouver: UBC Press.

Brown, Wendy. 1995. *States of Injury: Power and Freedom in Late Modernity*. Princeton: Princeton University Press.

Bullock, Katherine. 2002. *Rethinking Muslim Women and the Veil: Challenging Historical and Modern Stereotypes*. Herndon, VA: International Institute of Islamic Thought.

Butler, Judith. 1990, 1999, 2006. *Gender Trouble: Feminism and the Subversion of Identity*. New York and London: Routledge.

Butler, Judith. 1991. "Imitation and Gender Insubordination." In Diana Fuss, ed. *Inside/Out: Lesbian Theories, Gay Theories*. New York and London: Routledge, 13–31.

Butler, Judith. 1992. "Contingent Foundations." In Judith Butler and Joan W. Scott, ed. *Feminists Theorize the Political*. New York: Routledge, 3–21.

Butler, Judith. 1993. *Bodies That Matter: On the Discursive Limits of "Sex."* New York: Routledge.

Butler, Judith. 1999. *The Psychic Life of Power: Theories in Subjection*. Stanford: Stanford University Press.

Butler, Judith. 2005. *Giving An Account of Oneself*. New York: Fordham University Press.

Butler, Judith. 2009. "The Sensibility of Critique: Response to Asad and Mahmood." In Talal Asad, Wendy Brown, Judith Butler, Saba Mahmood, *Is Critique Secular? Blasphemy, Injury, and Free Speech*. Berkeley: University of California Press, 101–36.

Calhoun, Cheshire. 2000. *Feminism, the Family, and the Politics of the Closet: Lesbian and Gay Displacement*. New York: Oxford University Press.

Calhoun, Cheshire. 2008. "Losing Oneself," in Catriona MacKenzie and Kim Atkins, ed. *Practical Identity and Narrative Agency*. New York: Routledge, 193–211.

Castoriadis, Cornelius. 1997. "Logic, Imagination, Reflection." In *World in Fragments: Writings on Politics, Society, Psychoanalysis, and Imagination*. Ed. and trans. David Ames Curtis. Stanford, CA: Stanford University Press, 246–72.

Cavarero, Adriana. 2000. *Relating Narratives: Storytelling and Selfhood*. Trans. Paul A. Kottman. London and New York: Routledge.

Code, Lorraine. 1995. *Rhetorical Spaces: Essays on Gendered Locations*. New York: Routledge.

Cohen, Joshua, M. Howard, M. C. Nussbaum, ed. Susan Moller Okin with Respondents. 1999. *Is Multiculturalism Bad For Women?* Princeton, NJ: Princeton University Press.

Cole, Anna, Julia Burke and Winnie Woods. 1998. "Ngaanyatarra Pitjantjatjara Yankunytjatjara Women's Council." In Barbara Caine, ed. *Australian Feminism: A Companion*. Melbourne: Oxford University Press, .

Collins, Patricia Hill. 1990. *Black Feminist Thought: Knowledge, Consciousness, and the Politics of Empowerment*. London: HarperCollins.

Coole, Diana and Samantha Frost, ed. 2010. *New Materialisms: Ontology, Agency, and Politics*. Duke University Press.

Crenshaw, Kimberlé. 1991. "Mapping the Margins: Intersectionality, Identity Politics, and Violence Against Women of Color." *Stanford Law Review*. 43. (6): 1241–99.

Dean, Jodi. 1996. *Solidarity of Strangers: Feminism after Identity Politics*. Berkeley: University of California Press.

de Lauretis, Teresa. 1986. "Feminist Studies/Critical Studies: Issues, Terms, Contexts." In *Feminist Studies/Critical Studies,* ed. Teresa de Lauretis. Bloomington: Indiana University Press, 1–19.

de Lauretis, Teresa. 1987. *Technologies of Gender: Essays on Theory, Film, and Fiction*. Bloomington: University of Indiana Press.

de Lauretis, Teresa. 1990. "Eccentric Subjects: Feminist Theory and Historical Consciousness." *Feminist Studies* 16 (1): 115–50.

Descombes, Vincent. 1982. *Modern French Philosophy*. Trans. L. Scott-Fox and J. M. Harding. Cambridge: Cambridge University Press.

Dews, Peter . 1989. "The Return of the Subject in the Late Foucault." *Radical Philosophy* 51: 37–41.

Eisenberg, Avigail and Jeff Spinner-Halev. 2005. *Minorities Within Minorities: Equality, Rights and Diversity*. Cambridge: Cambridge University Press.

Fausto-Sterling, Anne. 1992. *Myths of Gender: Biological Theories about Women and Men*. New York: Basic Books.

Fausto-Sterling, Anne. 2000. *Sexing the Body: Gender Politics and the Construction of Sexuality*. New York: Basic Books.

Feinberg, Leslie. 1992. *Transgender Liberation: A Movement Whose Time Has Come*. New York: World View Forum.

Ferguson, Ann. 1995. "Feminist Communities and Moral Revolution." In *Feminism and community*, ed. Penny A. Weiss and Marilyn Friedman. Philadelphia: Temple University Press, 367–98.

Ferguson, Ann. 2000. "Resisting the Veil of Privilege: Building Bridge Identities as an Ethico-Politics of Global Feminisms." In *Decentering the Center: Philosophy for a Multicultural, Postcolonial, and Feminist World*. Ed. Uma Narayan and Sandra Harding. Bloomington: Indiana University Press, 189–207.

Foucault, Michel. 1978. *The History of Sexuality. Volume 1. An Introduction*. Trans. Robert Hurley. New York: Vintage.

Foucault, Michel. 1979. Discipline and Punish: The Birth of the Prison. Trans. Alan Sheridan. New York: Vintage.

Foucault, Michel. 1980a. "Truth and Power." In Power/Knowledge. Ed. Colin Gordon. New York: Pantheon.

Foucault, Michel. 1980b. Herculin Barbin, Being the Recently Discovered Memoirs of a Nineteenth Century French Hermaphrodite. Trans. Richard McDongall. New York: Pantheon.

Foucault, Michel. 1984a. "What is Enlightenment?" In The Foucault Reader. Ed. Paul Rabinow. New York: Pantheon, 32–50.

Foucault, Michel. 1984b. "On the Genealogy of Ethics: An Overview of Work in Progress." In *The Foucault Reader*. Ed. Paul Rabinow. New York: Pantheon, 340–72.

Foucault, Michel. 1986. The Care of the Self: The History of Sexuality. Volume 3. Trans. Robert Hurley. New York: Vintage.

Foucault, Michel. 1997a "The Ethics of Concern for the Self as a Practice of Freedom." In *Ethics: Subjectivity and Truth: Essential Works of Foucault*. Volume 1. Ed. Paul Rabinow. New York: The New Press, 281–302.

Foucault, Michel. 1997b "Sex, Power, and the Politics of Identity." In Ethics: Subjectivity and Truth. Essential Works of Foucault. Volume 1. Ed. Paul Rabinow. New York: The New Press, 163–174.

Foucault, Michel. 2000. "The Subject and Power." In *Power. Essential Works of Foucault*. Volume 3. Ed. James D. Faubion. New York: The New Press, 326–48.

Frankfurt, Harry. 1988. *The Importance of What We Care About*. Cambridge: Cambridge University Press.

Fraser, Nancy. 1997. "From Redistribution to Recognition? Dilemmas of Justice in a 'Postsocialist' Age." In *Justice Interruptus: Critical Reflections on the "Postsocialist" Condition*. New York and London: Routledge, 11–40.

Fraser, Nancy. 2010. *Scales of Justice: Reimagining Political Space in a Globalizing World*. New York: Columbia University Press.

Fraser, Nancy and Linda Gordon. 1994. "A Genealogy of 'Dependency': Tracing a Keyword of the U.S. Welfare State." *Signs* 19, (2): 309–36. Reprinted in Fraser, Nancy. *Justice Interruptus*. New York: Routledge, 1997.

Friedman, Marilyn. 2002. *Autonomy, Gender, Politics*. New York: Oxford University Press.

Frye, Marilyn. 1996. "The Necessity of Differences: Constructing a Positive Category of Women." *Signs: Journal of Women in Culture and Society* 21 (3): 991–1010.

Frye, Marilyn. 2005. "Categories in Distress." *Feminist Interventions in Ethics and Politics*. Ed. Barbara Andrew, Jean Keller, Lisa Schwartzman. Rowman and Littlefield.

Gatens, Moira. 1996. *Imaginary Bodies: Ethics, Power, and Corporeality*. London: Routledge.

Gibson-Graham, J.K. 2006. *A Postcapitalist Politics*. Minneapolis: University of Minnesota Press.

Grewal, Inderpal, and Caren Kaplan, eds. 1994. *Scattered Hegemonies: Postmodernity and Transnational Feminist Practices*. Minneapolis: University of Minnesota Press.

Grimshaw, Jean. 1993. "Practices of Freedom." In Caroline Ramazanoglu ed. *Up Against Foucalt*. New York and London: Routledge.

Grosz, Elizabeth. 1984/1985. Interview with Gayatri Spivak. *Thesis Eleven* 10: 1.

Grosz, Elizabeth. 1994. *Volatile Bodies: Toward a Corporeal Feminism*. Bloomington: Indiana University Press.

Güllen, Fethullah. 2007. *Key Concepts in the Practice of Sufism*. Volume 2. Fairfax, Virginia: The Fountain Press.

Habermas, Jürgen. 1979. "Historical Materialism and the Development of Normative Structures." In *Communication and the Evolution of Society*. Trans. Thomas McCarthy. Boston: Beacon Press, 95–129.

Haslanger, Sally. 2000. "Feminism and Metaphysics: Negotiating the Natural." In *The Cambridge Companion to Feminist Philosophy*. Ed. Miranda Fricker and Jennifer Hornsby. Cambridge: Cambridge University Press: 102–126.

Heinämaa, Sara. 2003. *Toward a Phenomenology of Sexual Difference: Husserl, Merleau-Ponty, Beauvoir*. Lanham: Rowman & Littlefield.

Hekman, Susan. 2005. *Private Selves, Public Identities: Reconsidering Identity Politics*. Penn State University Press.

Held, Virginia. 1987. "Non-contractual Society: A Feminist View." *Science, Morality, and Feminist Theory*. Ed. Marsha Hanen and Kai Nielsen. *Canadian Journal of Philosophy*, Supplementary Volume 13. Calgary: University of Calgary Press.

Held, Virginia. 1993. *Feminist Morality: Transforming Culture, Society, and Politics*. Chicago: University of Chicago Press.

Heyes, Cressida J. 2000. *Line Drawings: Defining Women through Feminist Practice*. Ithaca and London: Cornell University Press.

Heyes, Cressida J. 2007. *Self-Transformations: Foucault, Ethics, and Normalized Bodies*. New York: Oxford University Press.

Heyes, Cressida J. 2011. "Identity Politics." *Stanford Encyclopedia of Philosophy*.

Hirschmann, Nancy J. 2003. *The Subject of Liberty. Toward a Feminist Theory of Freedom*. Princeton: Princeton University Press.

Hirschkind, Charles. 1997. "What is Political Islam?" *Middle East Report* 27 (4): 12–14.

Hobbes, Thomas. 1982. *Leviathan*. Ed. C.B. Macpherson. New York: Viking.

Hochschild, Arlie Russell. 2000. Global care chains and emotional surplus value. In *Global Capitalism*, ed. Will Hutton and Anthony Giddens. New York: W. W. Norton.

Hochschild, Arlie Russell. 2002. Love and Gold. In *Global Woman*, ed. Barbara Ehrenreich and Arlie Russell Hochschild. New York: Metropolitan Books, 15-30.

Honig, Bonnie. 1994. Difference, Dilemmas, and the Politics of Home. *Social Research* 61 (3): 563–97.

hooks, bell. 1984. *Feminist Theory: From Margin to Centre*. Boston: South End Press.

hooks, bell. 1990. "Homeplace: A site of resistance." In *Yearning: Race, Gender, and Cultural Politics*. Boston: South End Press, 41–50.

Irigaray, Luce. 1992. *Ethics of sexual difference*. Ithaca, N.Y.: Cornell University Press.

Jaggar, Alison. 2000. "Globalizing Feminist Ethics." In Uma Narayan and Sandra Harding, ed. *Decentering the Center,* 1–25.

Jaggar, Alison, ed. 2009. "Special Issue on Global Gender Justice." *Philosophical Topics*. 37. 1.

Johnson-Odim, Cheryl. 1991. "Common Themes, Different contexts. Third World Women and Feminism." In *Third World Women and the Politics of Feminism*, ed. Chandra Talpade Mohanty, Ann Russo, and Lourdes Torres . Bloomington: Indiana University Press, 314–27.

Kristeva, Julia. 1991. *Strangers to Ourselves*. Trans. Leon S. Roudiez. New York: Columbia University Press.

Kruks, Sonia. 2001. *Retrieving Experience: Subjectivity and Recognition in Feminist Politics*. Ithaca: Cornell University Press.

Lazreg, Marnia. 2009. *Questioning the Veil: Open Letters to Muslim Women*. Princeton, NJ: Princeton University Press.

Lugones, María. 2003. "Playfulness, 'world'-traveling, and loving perception." In *Pilgrimages/Peregrinajes: Theorizing Coalition Against Multiple Oppressions*. Lanham, Md.: Rowman & Littlefield.

Lugones, Maria C. and Elizabeth V. Spelman. 1983. "Have We Got a Theory for You! Feminist Theory, Cultural Imperialism, and the Demand for 'The Woman's Voice.'" *Women's Studies International Forum*. 6. (6): 573–581.

Mackenzie, Catriona, and Natalie Stoljar, ed. 2000. *Relational autonomy: Feminist perspectives on autonomy, agency, and the social self*. Oxford: Oxford University Press.

Mackenzie, Catriona and Kim Atkins, ed. 2008. *Practical Identity and Narrative Agency*. New York: Routledge.

MacKinnon, Catharine A. 1982. "Feminism, Marxism, Method and the State: An Agenda for Theory," in Nannerl O. Keohane, Michelle Z. Rosaldo, and Barbara C. Gelpi, ed. *Feminist Theory: A Critique of Ideology*. Chicago: University of Chicago Press, 1–30.

MacKinnon, Catharine A. 1987. *Feminism Unmodified: Discourses on Life and Law*. Cambridge: Harvard University Press.

Mahmood, Saba. 2005. *Politics of Piety: The Islamic Revival and the Feminist Subject*. Princeton University Press.

Mahmood, Saba. 2009. "Religious Reason and Secular Affect: An Incommensurable Divide?" In Talal Asad, Wendy Brown, Judith Butler, Saba Mahmood, *Is Critique Secular? Blasphemy, Injury, and Free Speech*. Berkeley: University of California Press, 64–100.

Martin, Biddy. "Sexualities Without Genders and Other Queer Utopias." *diacritics* 24, (2–3) (1994): 104–121.

Martin, Biddy, and Chandra Talpade Mohanty. 1986. Feminist Politics: What's Home Got To Do with It? In *Feminist Studies/Critical Studies*, Teresa de Lauretis, ed. Bloomington: Indiana University Press, 191–212.

Marx, Karl. 1844. "Alienated Labour." In *Karl Marx: Early Writings*, trans. and ed. T. B. Bottomore. New York: McGraw-Hill.

McLaren, Margaret A. 1997. "Foucault and the Subject of Feminism." *Social Theory and Practice* 23, 1: 109-128.

McNay, Lois. 1992. *Foucault and Feminism: Power, Gender and the Self*. Boston: Northeastern University Press.

McNay, Lois. 2008. *Against Recognition*. Cambridge: Polity Press.

McWhorter, Ladelle. 2004. "Practicing, Practicing." In Dianna Taylor and Karen Vintges, ed. *Feminism and the Final Foucault*. Urbana: University of Illinois, 143–62.

Medina, José. 2003. "Identity Trouble: Disidentification and the Problem of Difference." *Philosophy and Social Criticism* 29 (6): 655–80.

Medina, José. 2006. *Speaking from Elsewhere: A New Contextualist Perspective on Meaning, Identity, and Discursive Agency*. Albany: SUNY.

Mernissi, Fatima. 1992. *The Veil and the Male Elite: A Feminist Interpretation of Women's Rights in Islam*. New York: Basic Books.

Mernissi, Fatima. 2001. *Scheherazade Goes West: Different Cultures, Different Harems*. New York: Washington Square Press.

Meyers, Diana Tietjens. 1989. *Self, Society and Personal Choice*. New York: Columbia University Press.

Meyers, Diana Tietjens. 2004. "Intersectional Identity and the Authentic Self? Opposites Attract!" In *Being Yourself: Essays on Identity, Action, and Social Life*. Lanham: Rowman and Littlefield.

Milan Women's Bookstore Collective. 1990. *Sexual Difference: A Theory of Social-Symbolic Practice*. Trans. Patricia Cicogna and Teresa de Lauretis. Bloomington: Indiana University Press.

Mill, John Stuart. 1859. *On liberty*. London: John W. Parker & Son.

Mills, Charles W. 1997. *The Racial Contract*. Ithaca: Cornell University Press.

Moghadam, Valentine M . 1994a. *Identity politics and women: Cultural reassertions and feminisms in international perspective*. Boulder, Colo.: Westview.

Moghadam, Valentine M. 1994b. *Gender and National Identity: Women and Politics in Muslim Societies*. NJ.: Zed Books.

Mohanty, Chandra Talpade. 1987. Feminist encounters: Locating the politics of experience. *Copyright* 1 (Fall): 30–44.

Mohanty, Chandra Talpade. 2003. *Feminism without borders: Decolonizing theory, practicing solidarity*. Durham, NC.: Duke University Press.

Mohanty, Chandra Talpade, Ann Russo, and Lourdes Torres, ed. 1991. *Third World Women and the Politics of Feminism*. Bloomington: Indiana University Press.

Mohanty, Satya P. 1989. Us and them: On the philosophical bases of political criticism. *Yale Journal of Criticism* 2 (Spring): 1–31.

Mohanty, Satya P. 1993. "The Epistemic Status of Cultural Identity: On Beloved and the Postcolonial Condition." *Cultural Critique* 24: 41–80.

Mohanty, Satya P. 1997. *Literary Theory and the Claims of History: Postmodernism, Objectivity, Multicultural Politics*. Ithaca: Cornell University Press.

Moi, Toril. 1999. *What is a Woman?* Oxford: Oxford University Press.

Moraga, Cherrie and Gloria Anzaldúa, ed. 1981. *This Bridge Called My Back: Writings by Radical Women of Color*. New York: Kitchen Table Press.

Morrison, Toni. 1987. *Beloved*. New York: Random House.

Mouffe, Chantal. 1992. "Democratic politics today." In *Dimensions of Radical Democracy: Pluralism, Citizenship, Community*. London: Verso.

Moya, Paula M.L . 2000a. "Introduction: Reclaiming Identity." Paula M. L. Moya and Michael Hames-Garcia. *Reclaiming Identity: Realist Theory and the Predicament of Postmodernism*. Berkeley and Los Angeles: University of California Press, 1–26.

Moya, Paula M. L. 2000b. "Postmodernism, "Realism," and the Politics of Identity: Cherrîe Moraga and Chicana Feminism." Paula M. L. Moya and Michael Hames-Garcia. *Reclaiming Identity: Realist Theory and the Predicament of Postmodernism*. Berkeley and Los Angeles: University of California Press, 67–101.

Moya, Paula M.L. 2002. *Learning from experience: Minority identities, multicultural struggles*. Berkeley and Los Angeles: University of California Press.

Moya, Paula M. L. and Michael Hames-Garcia. 2000. *Reclaiming Identity: Realist Theory and the Predicament of Postmodernism*. Berkeley and Los Angeles: University of California Press.

Muñoz, José E. 1999. *Disidentifications: Queers of Color and the Performance of Politics*. Minneapolis: University of Minnesota Press.

Narayan, Uma. 1997. *Dislocating Cultures: Identities, Traditions, and Third World Feminism*. New York: Routledge.

Narayan, Uma. 2000. "Essence of Culture and a Sense of History." In *Decentering the Center: Philosophy for a Multicultural, Postcolonial, and Feminist World*. Ed. Uma Narayan and Sandra Harding. Bloomington: Indiana University Press, 80–100.

Narayan, Uma and Sandra Harding, ed. (2000). *Decentering the Center: Philosophy for a Multicultural, Postcolonial, and Feminist World*. Bloomington: Indiana University Press.

Nedelsky, Jennifer. 1989. "Reconceiving Autonomy: Sources, Thoughts and Possibilities." *Yale Journal of Law and Feminism* 1: (7): 7–36.

Nedelsky, Jennifer. 2011. *Law's Relations: A Relational Theory of Self, Autonomy, and Law*. Oxford: Oxford University Press.

Nicholson, Linda. 1994. "Interpreting Gender." *Signs: Journal of Women in Culture and Society* 20: 79–105.

Nicholson, Linda. 2008. *Identity Before Identity Politics*. Cambridge: Cambridge University Press.

Nicholson, Linda. 2010. "Identity After Identity Politics." *Washington University Journal of Law and Policy*. 33: 43.

Nouraie-Simone, Fereshteh. 2005. *On Shifting Ground: Muslim Women in the Global Era*. New York: The Feminist Press at CUNY.

Okin, Susan Moller. 2000. "Feminism, Women's Human Rights, and Cultural Differences." In *Decentering the Center: Philosophy for a Multicultural, Postcolonial, and Feminist World*. Ed. Uma Narayan and Sandra Harding. Bloomington: Indiana University Press.

Oliver, Kelly. 2001. *Witnessing: Beyond Recognition*. Minneapolis: University of Minnesota.

Pettit, Philip. 1997. *Republicanism: A Theory of Freedom and Government*. Oxford: Oxford University Press.

Phelan, Shane. 1989. *Identity politics: Lesbian Feminism and the Limits of Community*. Philadelphia: Temple University Press.

Phillips, Anne. 2009. *Multiculturalism Without Culture*. Princeton, NJ: Princeton University Press.

Pratt, Minnie Bruce. 1988. "Identity: Skin Blood Heart." In Elly Bulkin, Minnie Bruce Pratt, and Barbara Smith. *Yours In Struggle: Three Feminist Perspectives on Anti-Semitism and* Racism. Ithaca, N.Y.: Firebrand Books, 9–63.

Prosser, Jay. 1998. *Second Skins: The Body Narratives of Transsexuality*. New York: Columbia University Press.

Radicalesbians. 1973. The Woman-Identified Woman. In *Radical Feminism*, ed. Anne Koedt, Ellen Levine, and Anita Rapone. New York: Times Books.

Razack, Sherene. 2008. *Casting Out: The Eviction of Muslims from Western Law and Politics*. Toronto: University of Toronto Press.

Reagon, Bernice Johnson. 1983. Coalition politics: Turning the century. In *Home Girls: A Black Feminist Anthology*, ed. Barbara Smith. New York: Kitchen Table, Women of Color Press. Reprinted by Rutgers University Press.

Rich, Adrienne. 1980. "Compulsory Heterosexuality and Lesbian Existence." *Signs: Journal of Women in Culture and Society* 5 (4): 631–90.

Ricoeur, Paul. 1970. *Freud and Philosophy: An Essay on Interpretation*. Trans. Denis Savage. New Haven: Yale University Press.

Riley, Denise. 1988. "*Am I that name?" Feminism and the category of "women" in history*. Minneapolis: University of Minnesota.

Rose, Jacqueline. 1986. *Sexuality in the Field of Vision*. London: Verso.

Rubin, Gayle. 1975. "The Traffic in Women: Notes on the 'Political Economy' of Sex." In Rayna Reiter, ed., *Toward an Anthropology of Women*. New York: Monthly Review Press.

Ruddick, Sara. 1989. "Preservative Love." In *Maternal thinking: Toward a Politics of Peace*. New York: Ballantine Books.

Sawicki, Jana. 1991. *Disciplining Foucault*. New York and London: Routledge.

Schachar, Ayelet. 2001. *Multicultural Jurisdictions: Cultural Differences and Women's Rights*. Cambridge: Cambridge University Press.

Scheman, Naomi. 1997. "Queering the Center by Centering the Queer: Reflections on Transsexuals and Secular Jews." In Diana Tietjens Meyers, ed. *Feminists Rethink the Self*. Boulder: Westview Press, 124–62.

Scheman, Naomi. 2011. *Shifting Ground. Knowledge and Reality, Transgression and Trustworthiness*. New York: Oxford University Press.

Scott, Joan Wallach. 2007. *The Politics of the Veil*. Princeton, NJ: Princeton University Press.

Sedgwick, Eve Kosofsky. 1990. *Epistemology of the Closet*. Berkeley: University of California Press.

Shohat, Ella. 2001. *Talking Visions: Multicultural Feminism in a Transnational Age*. Cambridge: MIT Press

Skinner, Quentin. 2002. "A Third Concept of Liberty." *Proceedings of the British Academy* 117, 237–268.

Smith, Zadie. 2000. *White Teeth*. London: Hamish Hamilton.

Spelman, Elizabeth V. 1988. *Inessential Woman: Problems of Exclusion in Feminist Thought*. Boston: Beacon Press.

Stryker, Susan and Stephen Whittle, ed. 2006. *The Transgender Studies Reader*. New York: Routledge.

Taylor, Charles. 1985a. *Human Agency and Language: Philosophical Papers vol*.1. Cambridge: Cambridge University Press.

Taylor, Charles. 1985b. What's Wrong With Negative Liberty. *Philosophy and the Human Sciences: Philosophical Papers* vol. 2, 211-229.. Cambridge: Cambridge University Press.

Taylor, Charles. 1989. *Sources of the Self: The Making of the Modern Identity*. Cambridge, Mass.: Harvard University Press.

Taylor, Charles. 1992. "The Politics of Recognition." In *Multiculturalism and "The Politics of Recognition"*. Ed. Amy Gutmann. Princeton, NJ: Princeton University Press, 25–74.

Taylor, Charles. 2007. *A Secular Age*. Cambridge, Mass.: Harvard University Press.

Tronto, Joan. 1992. *Moral Boundaries*. New York: Routledge.

Taylor, Dianna and Karen Vintges, ed. 2004. *Feminism and the Final Foucault*. Urbana: University of Illinois.

Tully, James. 1995. *Strange Multiplicity: Constitutionalism in an Age of Diversity*. Cambridge: Cambridge University Press.

Tully, James. 2008. *Public Philosophy in a New Key. Volume 1: Democracy and Civic Freedom*. Cambridge: Cambridge University Press.

Uttal, Lynet. 1990. Nods that Silence. In *Making Face, Making Soul: Haciendo Caras: Creative and Critical Perspectives by Feminists of Color*. Ed. Gloria Anzaldúa. San Francisco: Aunt Lute Books.

Wadud, Amina. 1999. *Qur'an and Woman: Rereading the Sacred Text from a Woman's Perspective*. New York: Oxford University Press.

Wadud, Amina. 2006. *Inside the Gender Jihad: Women's Reform in Islam*. London: Oneworld Publications.

Warnke, Georgia. 2007. *After Identity: Rethinking Race, Sex and Gender*. Cambridge: Cambridge University Press.

Weir, Allison. 1995. "Toward a Model of Self-Identity: Habermas and Kristeva." In Johanna Meehan, ed. *Feminists Read Habermas: Gendering the Subject of Discourse*. New York: Routledge, 263–82.

Weir, Allison. 1996. *Sacrificial Logics: Feminist Theory and the Critique of Identity*. New York and London: Routledge.

Weir, Allison. 2005. "The Global Universal Caregiver: Imagining Women's Liberation in the Third Millenium," *Constellations: An International Journal of Critical and Democratic Theory*, 12, (3): 308–30.

West, Cornel. 1995. "A Matter of Life and Death." In *The Identity in Question*, ed. John Rajchman. New York: Routledge, 147–71.

Wideman, John Edgar. 1999. Interviewed in Judgment Day, episode 4 of *Africans in America* on PBS.

Willett, Cynthia. 2001. *The Soul of Justice: Social Bonds and Racial Hubris*. Ithaca, N.Y.: Cornell University Press.

Willett, Cynthia. 2008. "Three Concepts of Freedom." In *Irony in the Age of Empire: Comic Perspectives on Democracy and Freedom*. Bloomington: Indiana University Press.

Wittig, Monique. 1992. "One is Not Born a Woman." In *The Straight Mind*. Boston: Beacon Press.

Woolf, Virginia. 1928. *A Room of One's Own*. London: Hogarth Press.

Young, Iris Marion. 1990. "City Life and Difference." In *Justice and the Politics of Difference*. Princeton, N.J.: Princeton University Press.

Young, Iris Marion. 1997a. "House and Home: Feminist Variations on a Theme." In *Intersecting voices: Dilemmas of Gender, Political Philosophy, and Policy*. Princeton, N.J.: Princeton University Press.

Young, Iris Marion. 1997b. Mothers, Citizenship, and Independence: A Critique of Pure Family Values. In *Intersecting Voices: Dilemmas of Gender, Political Philosophy, and Policy*. Princeton, N.J.: Princeton University Press.

Young, Iris Marion. 1997c. "Communication and the Other: Beyond Deliberative Democracy." In *Intersecting voices: Dilemmas of Gender, Political Philosophy, and Policy*. Princeton, N.J.: Princeton University Press.

Young, Iris Marion. 2000. *Inclusion and Democracy*. Oxford: Oxford University Press.

Young, Iris Marion. 2002. "Autonomy, Welfare Reform, and Meaningful Work." In *The subject of care: Feminist perspectives on dependency*, ed. Eva Feder Kittay and Ellen K. Feder. Lanham, Md.: Rowman & Littlefield, 40–60.

Young, Iris Marion. 2005. "A Room of One's own: Old Age, Extended Care, and Privacy." *In On Female Body Experience*. New York: Oxford University Press.

Young, Iris Marion. 2007. *Global Challenges: War, Self-Determination and Responsibility for Justice*. Polity Press.

Zerilli, Linda. 2005. *Feminism and the Abyss of Freedom*. Chicago: University of Chicago Press.

Ziarek, Ewa. 2001. *An Ethics of Dissensus: Postmodernity, Feminism, and the Politics of Radical Democracy*. Stanford: Stanford University Press.

INDEX

Abir, 143–44
Abu-Lughod, Lila, 118
Adorno, Theodor, 87
affectional solidarity, 81, 85n13
"Against Proper Objects" (Butler), 96
agency
  Butler and, 120, 122, 125–26
  in feminist politics, 74, 120
  Foucault and, 120, 123, 125–26,
    130–32, 148n9
  freedom and, 10–11, 120, 123, 125–26,
    130–32
  as inhabiting norms, 10, 14, 130–35
  in Islamic revival, 19, 120–33, 136–37,
    140, 143
  Mahmood and, 19, 20n9, 120–29
  multiple relations in, 6
  resistance and, 10–11
  women and, 104–6
Ahmed, Leila, 135
Ahmed, Sara, 97–98
Alcoff, Linda, 1, 12, 31, 65–67, 89, 116n5
"Alienated Labour" (Marx), 58
alienation, 11–12, 35, 37
Allen, Amy, 88, 20n10, 44n12, 148n9,
  149n26
Allen, Anita, 49, 55, 61n5
alternative communities, 28
Althusser, Louis, 7
Anzaldua, Gloria, 80
Arendt, Hannah
  on work, 58

Zerilli and, 14, 102, 104–6, 109–10,
  114–15, 120
asocial ethics, 41
authenticity
  Foucault and, 25–26
  freedom and, 28
  ideal of, 25–26, 42n2, 141
  intersectional identities and, 42n2
  quest for, 15, 22, 25, 28, 31
  question, 32–33
  social identities and, 26–27
  Taylor and, 15, 22, 25–26, 28, 31, 141
autonomy
  as positive freedom, 61n7
  privacy and, 54–56
  relational, 17, 61n10, 140

Baier, Annette, 43n6
barred rooms, identities as, 76
Beauvoir, Simone de, 58–59, 87, 118, 119
belonging
  freedom as, 33–42, 118–47
  "Samad Iqbal" and, 22, 34, 39
Beloved (Morrison), 57
Benhabib, Seyla, 71, 129
Berlin, Isaiah, 145, 149n25, 154
best account principle, 35
binding identities, danger of, 62
black women
  Reagon and, 74–75
  single mothers on welfare, 15, 23, 27,
    30, 35